"Derick Sebastian is an artist who defines being professional as not good but great. I call this difference the 'IT' factor. His warmth, passion, genuine love for life, and professional excellence draw the audience to gratitude and happiness. Derick Sebastian is a miracle."

— Fred Crowell
Visionary, Founder, President, NBC Camps

"Derick's music comes from his heart and, in turn, will touch yours."

— Ricky Nierva
Production and Creative Designer, Filmmaker, and Storyteller

"In my years of entertainment, no one has captured my attention as much as Derick Sebastian! He's not only a maestro ukulele genius, but a very polished vocalist. There are many great ukulele masters, but Derick is the very best at the top above all. He's truly a blessed and talented man."

— Willie Kahaiali'i
International Performing Artist, Writer, and Producer

"Derick is an inspiration with his commitment to precision in playing the ukulele! I have found his devotion to the music and ukulele world are unmatched."

— Jeff Rafner
Producer and Production Manager

"Taking an ukulele lesson with Derick was such a fun experience. He has something special to offer musicians of every level!"

— Jesse Carmichael
Maroon 5, Artist, Writer, Producer, and Composer

"Derick is an incredibly inspiring human whose passion and dedication shine through in everything he does. His genuine kindness and unwavering commitment to empowering others make him a true beacon of positivity. I'm constantly amazed by his ability to touch lives and motivate those around him to pursue their dreams with confidence."

— Kris Bradley
Creator and Founder of Produce Like a Boss, Producer,
Singer, and Songwriter

"Derick Sebastian is one of the coolest ukulele artists in Hawaii. His musical style is unlike any other! His fingers float across the fretboard effortlessly with soothing harmonics and a gentle touch. Derick's heartwarming Aloha and gift of music is where he is able to capture the magical spirit of storytelling. A true artist who honors his family and gives the glory to God."

— Johnson Enos
Creator and Composer of *Honu by the Sea: The Musical*

"It was one thing to know Derick is an ukulele virtuoso. It was another to experience the palpable joy Derick had on his face while teaching our entire family. He literally had a smile on his face the entire time and made our time together that much more enjoyable. Plus, within thirty minutes, he had us all strumming to a song that someone walking by could actually name. We all know the teacher makes the difference. Derick Sebastian is that kind of teacher."

— Mark Stevenett
Vice President, Love Communications

"Listening to Derick Sebastian play the ukulele is truly an exceptional experience. He plays with such clarity and heart that it's truly remarkable."

— Patrick Ewing, Jr.
Coach, GM, and Former NBA and International Pro Basketball Player

"Derick Sebastian is the complete artist, talented and beyond, while remaining personable and humble."

— Claytoven Richardson
Grammy Award-Winning Artist, Songwriter,
Producer, Educator, and Author

"Derick is a unique performer who always leaves the crowd wanting more. His musical talents and contagious spirit are something everyone should have the chance to enjoy firsthand."

— Will Posthumus
Production Creative, Producer, Filmmaker

"While on a family trip to Maui, we were captivated by Derick's music and became big fans not only because of his talent, but also for his kindness, compassion, sincerity, and infectious personality. We have been friends since, and I've had him perform the national anthem at our home games so our fans could experience his charismatic soul and love of life."

— Derrick Hall
President and CEO, Arizona Diamondbacks

"Derick has a beautiful gift of making everyone feel like family. He has never met a stranger! As our wedding officiant, he made our wedding day the most beautiful day, and we will be forever thankful to him for his perfect words on our big day."

— Griffin and Amanda Mazur
Clemson Tigers Baseball Assistant Coach and Former D1 Baseball Player
USA Softball Gold Medalist and Former D1 Softball Player


"I've taken lessons from many ukulele and guitar teachers. I had given up on being able to grasp methods and techniques until I met Derick. After the first lesson, I actually played my first song with moderate techniques. Derick is gifted as a player and teacher. He is patient and has a way about him that makes one want to play. I recommend him highly."

— George Keys
President, Keys Claims Consultants


"Derick is truly an exceptionally talented musician, but his character and how he lives his life is even more beautiful! His love for family, the planet, and those he doesn't even know shines so very brightly! He's always smiling and bringing joy to others, which in this world is, unfortunately, not something people do enough. I know Derick loves his life, feels gratitude for all he's worked hard for, and is a gorgeous human being, and for that, I'm absolutely honored to be his friend!"

— Chris Mollere
Music Supervisor, Fusion Music Supervision


"Derick Sebastian's ukulele journey is a true blessing to the world!"

— Anthony Tolliver
Former Professional Thirteen-Year NBA Veteran

"Derick has always been an outstanding musician with a love and dedication to his craft that radiates through him, as does his genuine heart and Spirit of Aloha."

— Justin Young
Songwriter, Producer, and Performer

"Derick Sebastian is, first and foremost, a wonderful human being and a true joy to work with. Not only is he a very talented and accomplished musician, but his creativity and ability to provide clients with exactly what they need exemplify true professionalism."

— Gabriel Candiani
Music Producer, Founder/Owner of Sky Urbano Music Library

"Derick is full of Aloha! He spent some time teaching ukulele to my grandkids and was very patient, loving, and encouraging. This world needs more people like Derick, who simply spread the Aloha Spirit."

— Chris Miles
Entrepreneur and Restaurant Owner, Cookin' on Wood, MLB Caterer

"You think time travel isn't possible? My friends, some magicians can bend time to their will, teasing it from strings with their fingertips, sending it to reach our souls through our ears. They help us feel the warmth of past moments and the hope of tomorrow. They make our minds and hearts race while making time stand still. Derick is one of these magicians of time, whose magic is music—a magician so powerful I suspect he's actually timeless."

— Scott Morse
Filmmaker and Graphic Novelist

"When my wife and I moved to Maui, we knew no one. A young fifteen-year-old local boy named Santana Sebastian reached out to me for an internship opportunity. I brought Santana onto a handful of projects and had never seen so much talent, maturity, and grace in such a young person before. It all made sense when I met his father, Derick. The attention, creativity, openness, and love Derick instills in his family is admirable and is reflected in his three boys. Derick extended that same love to my family, finally making Maui feel like home to us. Derick embodies what it means to live Aloha."

— Danny Gevirtz
Filmmaker, Director, and YouTube Creator

"I love Derick's spirit! He is such a passionate person, and you can feel it when he plays the ukulele—his heart is right out front. This book is another beautiful example of his heart expressed through his words. Enjoy the journey!"

— Ron Callan
Broadcaster, Oregon State Play-by-Play,
and PA Announcer Seattle Seahawks

"Derick Sebastian embodies the truth that passion drives purpose and with persistence anything can be conquered. You'll love the stories of how he not only began to play the ukulele but went on to play the national anthem at NBA and MLB games, go on international tours, and record albums. His willpower is beyond admirable, and his musical talent makes me think the old Hawaiian gods are smiling upon, and yet he remains just a humble man who plays the ukulele."

— Nicole Gabriel
Author of *Finding Your Inner Truth*
and *Stepping Into Your Becoming*

"Derick has always shown incredible kindness, not just to me but to everyone around him. Watching him perform is an absolute joy—his talent is undeniable, and the way he pours his soul into every note is truly captivating. His music has a way of touching the heart and uplifting the spirit."

—Mitchell Tenpenny
Country Pop Singer and Songwriter Star

"I've had the privilege of knowing Derick Sebastian since he was a young boy, just beginning his ukulele journey. Even then, it was clear he was destined for greatness. His talent was undeniable, but what truly stood out was the passion in his eyes—an unquenchable drive that assured me he would go far. Over the years, I've watched Derick grow, evolve, and reach incredible heights. From his unforgettable renditions of the national anthem at basketball games to his unique style that pushes the boundaries of the ukulele, he continues to impress. I've been a fan since day one and remain a fan to this day. I now wish Derick nothing but the best on his new journey as an author. The future holds even greater things for him, and I know God is guiding Derick every step of the way."

—Kelly Boy DeLima
Founder and Leader of the Musical Group Kapena,
Ukulele Virtuoso, and Entertainer

"Reading *Daydreaming With Purpose* is like listening to a symphony, all played by ukulele. Derick Sebastian shares the ups and downs of his musical journey, sharing hard-earned lessons. His unwavering positivity and willpower will inspire you to believe you can always achieve anything you focus on and are passionate about. This book deserves to win a Grammy."

— Tyler R. Tichelaar, PhD
Award-Winning Author of *Narrow Lives* and *The Best Place*

# WELCOME

I'm excited to have you here!

Scan the QR code below to access a special video that will inspire and empower you on this journey.

www.DerickSebastian.com

AN INSPIRATIONAL MEMOIR OF THE ALOHA SPIRIT IN ACTION

# DAYDREAMING
# WITH
# PURPOSE

## SELF-LEADERSHIP STRATEGIES TO MANIFEST
## YOUR PASSION INTO YOUR PROFESSION

*Derick Sebastian*

FOREWORD BY MICHAEL A. ACZON

SOUNDS OF SEBASTIAN
PUBLISHING

**DAYDREAMING WITH PURPOSE**
Self-Leadership Strategies to Manifest Your Passion into Your Profession

Derick Sebastian
Sounds of Sebastian, LLC
Sounds of Sebastian Publishing
PO Box 63
Wailuku, HI 96793
Office: (808) 870-8460
www.DaydreamingWithPurpose.com
www.DerickSebastian.com

For additional copies, visit:
www.DaydreamingWithPurpose.com

ISBN: 979-8-9916859-0-0 (hardcover)
979-8-9916859-1-7 (softcover)
Library of Congress # 2024922560

Book Coach/Project Manager: Patrick Snow
The Snow Group
Editing: Tyler Tichelaar
Superior Book Productions
Cover and Interior Book Design: Nicole Gabriel
Let's Get Your Book Published

Every attempt has been made to properly source all quotes.

Printed in the United States of America

First Edition

2 4 6 8 10 12

# DEDICATION

To God: My almighty Lord and Savior, whose unconditional love, grace, and guidance have been the foundation and truth of my life. Your blessings have made all things possible.

To my loving soulmate and wife Raymi: Thank you for your unwavering love, patience, and support.

To my three sons Santana, Marley, and Jackson: I'm forever grateful to be your dad. Thank you for being my *why* in life.

To my heavenly dad Rogelio (1943-1985): Thank you for being the rock of our entire family. I miss and think of you every day. Though we had limited time together here, I know we'll have eternity to catch up.

To my mom Dolores: You are my absolute hero! Thank you for always working hard and never giving up on our family.

To my siblings Rose, Roger, Debra, and Chris: Thank you for always being the best siblings I could ever have.

To my late *hanai* dad, dearest friend, and mentor Mr. Sam "Mister" Ellis (1965-2013): Your endless belief in me is a cornerstone of my success. I miss you so much. *Mahalo* for introducing me to the ukulele!

To my book coaches, creative consultants, and accountability partners Patrick Snow and Autumn Shields: Huge *mahalos* for believing in my vision, being my accountability partner, and helping me bring this book to life. Your expertise and guidance have been invaluable.

To all my readers, you: Thank you for taking the time to engage with my story. Your support and enthusiasm mean the world to me. I hope my journey inspires you to pursue your own dreams with passion and perseverance.

# ACKNOWLEDGMENTS

To my Chicago *ohana* Tom and Eileen English: Huge *mahalos* for always being my biggest cheerleaders! Your support is immeasurable.

To my extended Maui *ohana* Earl and Rochelle Inouye: Thank you for always believing in me and embracing me for who I am. Your invaluable life lessons, love, and support have helped me become who I am today.

To my Tennessee *ohana* Eddie and Stephanie Kim: Thank you for your endless love, light, and guidance. Family is everything!

To my executive creative manager Charhez Pulvera: You're a gift, a miracle. Thank you so much for all your endless hard work; you're immensely appreciated.

To my incredible super team: Rick Rasay, Irene Tsouprake Holombo, Johnson Enos, Kevin Jarc, Michael Aczon, Trisha Smith, Mark Hirabayashi, Lynne Kuraoka, and everyone involved in my production, creative process, and artist development—your unwavering encouragement, steadfast accountability, tireless hard work, and boundless dedication have turned every single one of my dreams into reality. I am profoundly grateful for your endless love, support, and invaluable contributions. Thank you for being the backbone of my journey and helping me achieve my artistic vision.

To my ukulele *ohana* Joe and Kristen of Kanile'a Ukuleles: Thank you for always being family and providing me with the best, most innovative ukuleles in the world.

To my music partners in crime Ryan Tanaka, John Palpallatoc, Josh Kahula, Dane Patao Jr., Dana Navarro Arias, Desmond Yap, Mahie Pokipala, Jason Pokipala, Jacob de la Nux, Jason Swann, and the boys of Malino. Mahalo, friends for all the good times in music and life. I surely wouldn't be here in my musical journey without you folks.

To my energetic, high-on-life vocal coach Joy Fields: Thank you for always believing in me and bringing out the best in me. It's truly a blessing to be your "champ."

To my creative hero Ricky Nierva: Thank you for your unconditional encouragement and inspiration. Automatic!

To my extended *ohana*—the Sebastians, Todas, Sensanos, Hifos, Hos, Panems, Kanihos, Houstons, Manuels, Begas, Sudas, Goos, Edlaos, Magbuals, Matsudas, and Spanglers: Thank you from the bottom of my heart. I'm forever grateful.

To the endless list of father figures, mentors, and accountability friends who have guided me: I know you know who you all are. Your love, mentorship, and wisdom shaped my journey and inspired me to pursue my dreams with passion and perseverance. *Mahalo* a million!

To my late uncle Henry "Aiau" Koa (1963-2021): *Mahalo* for always being there for me. You taught me how to live, laugh, and love. "What's up, Hawaiian?"

To my late ukulele hero Eddie Bush (1935-2002): Thank you for changing my life. "The best is yet to come."

To my late uncle Henry "Boy" Kanae—The Maui Hawaiian Superman (1953-2008): *Mahalo* for always showing me what living "Aloha" was all about. "If nothing goes right, then take it to the left."

To my late dear friend and artist development consultant, Tim Sweeney of Music Strategies (1964–2014): Thank you for transforming my mindset and inspiring me to dream big, pursue endless opportunities, and embrace my journey as an independent music artist.

To all my family, friends, and extended *ohana* across Hawaii and around the world: I live in pure gratitude because of you. What a true honor and blessing to represent you the best way I know how. Thank you from the bottom of my heart.

To my fellow artists, musicians, colleagues, and mentors in the creative industry all over the world: You know who you are—your encouragement and collaboration have been essential to my development as an artist. Thank you for sharing your wisdom and pushing me to reach new heights.

www.DerickSebastian.com

# SPECIAL ACKNOWLEDGMENTS

**People (*Ohana*)**

Alakai Paleka and *Ohana*, Alana Rucynski and *Ohana*, Angelique Eva Calvillo, Autumn Shields and Mike Tarantino, Ben and Tiffany Prangnell, Ben Benevente, Biff Gore and *Ohana*, Bill and Pat Schmitt, Billy Galewood, Branscombe Richmond and *Ohana*, Brittain Komoda, Carl Andrews and *Ohana*, Cecilia Mörnhed and *Ohana*, Chanelle "Coco" Urmeneta, Chris Miles and *Ohana*, Chris and Karen Harmening, Claytoven Richardson and *Ohana*, Craig Mauck and *Ohana*, Dale Nitta and *Ohana*, Dan and Claudia Goodfellow, Darlene and John Neu, Dave Barry and *Ohana*, David Kuraya and *Ohana*, Don McEntire and *Ohana*, Elliott Prestwich and *Ohana*, Emmett and Ranette Rodrigues, Eric Ely and *Ohana*, Erik Bateman, Gabe Kreuger and *Ohana*, Gabriel and Adassa Candiani, Genevie Mendoza, George Kahumoku and *Ohana*, George and Carol Keys, Glenn and Christy Soby, Isaac Bancaco and *Ohana*, Jan and Kelly Apo, Jason Mraz, Jeff Smith, Jeff and Mary Rafner, Jo Koy and *Ohana*, Joe Bustillos and *Ohana*, John and Cristina Graziano, John and Victoria Stewart, Johnette Lacno-Ellis, Johnny Walker and *Ohana*, Jon Marro, Kainoa Horcajo and *Ohana*, Kaliko Storer and *Ohana*, Keane Lee and *Ohana*, Kelly Boy DeLima and *Ohana*, Kim McEnaney and *Ohana*, Kipi Higa and *Ohana*, Kris Bradley, Kye and Jenissa Bolen, Larry Alexander, Lauren Trusty, Mark Baquial, Mark Fonseca and *Ohana*, Melvin Yagin and *Ohana*, Michael "Rahlo" Porter, Sr., Mike Bena and *Ohana*, Mike Fetters and *Ohana*, Nicole Gabriel, Patrick Snow and *Ohana*, Puka and Holly Ho, Rama Camarillo and *Ohana*, Roberta Means and *Ohana*, Ron Callan and *Ohana*, Ron Moss, Russel Amaral, Ryan and Caroline May, Sam Knaak and *Ohana*, Scott Rueck and *Ohana*, Sean Ramos and *Ohana*, Steven Laffoon and *Ohana*, Takushi *Ohana*, Tony Takitani and *Ohana*, Troy and Michelle Tardiville, Tyler Tichelaar, Vickie and Rick Jackson, Vince and Maggie Tuzzi, Waddy Dacay and *Ohana*, Wes Ignacio and *Ohana*, and Will Posthumus and *Ohana*.

## Businesses and Organizations

ABC Studios, All Pono, Analysis Plus Cables, Andaz Maui at Wailea, Anna Kim Photography, Anthony Martinez Photography, April Szabo Portrait Design, Countess Ukuleles and Guitars, Da Jam 98.3 FM, Duke's Kaanapali, Envisions Entertainment, Fishman, Fusion Bags, Hawaii News Now, Hawaii Songwriting Festival, HI92 Maui FM, *Honu by the Sea, The Musical,* Hope Chapel Maui, Hula Grill Kaanapali, KCCN FM100, KHON2 News, KITV 4 News, KPOA 93.5 FM, Kahului Elementary School, Kanile'a Ukuleles, Kimo's Restaurant Front Street, Loco Mango Ukuleles, Maui Arts and Cultural Center, Maui High School, Maui Invitational, Maui Songwriters Festival, Maui Waena Intermediate School, Mele Ukuleles, Na Hoku Hanohano Awards, Noelani's Grill, No Ka Oi Songwriters Festival, Oregon State University, Pixar Animation Studios, Pono's Hawaiian Grill, Q103 Maui FM, ROXY, Scott Drexler Photography, Sean Hower Photography, TEDx, and The Songwriting School of Los Angeles.


## Sports Teams and Organizations

Arizona Diamondbacks, Atlanta Braves, Chicago Cubs, Cincinnati Reds, Cleveland Cavaliers, EA SPORTS, ESPN, Los Angeles Angels, Los Angeles Clippers, Los Angeles Dodgers, Los Angeles Lakers, Major League Baseball, Memphis Grizzlies, Milwaukee Brewers, Minnesota Timberwolves, National Basketball Association, National Collegiate Athletics Association, Pittsburgh Pirates, Players Golf Association, San Diego Padres, San Francisco Giants, Seattle Mariners, Tampa Bay Rays, Texas Rangers, Utah Jazz, and Vertical Sports Maui.

www.DerickSebastian.com

www.DerickSebastian.com

# CONTENTS

Foreword:      Charting the Ocean of Dreams by Michael A. Aczon     27

Introduction:  Your Aloha Awakening                                 33

## SECTION 1:   PREPARING FOR YOUR JOURNEY                          39

Chapter 1:     Being Ready for Your "Go Time"                       45

Chapter 2:     Finding Your Home                                    59

Chapter 3:     Uncovering Your Hidden Blessings                     71

Chapter 4:     Getting in Your Game                                 83

## SECTION 2:   OVERCOMING YOUR CHALLENGES                          97

Chapter 5:     Breaking Your Broomstick                             103

Chapter 6:     Pursuing Your Unattainable Goals                     117

Chapter 7:     Mastering Your Biggest Challenges                    129

Chapter 8:     Navigating Your Life's Grief                         141

## SECTION 3:   BUILDING YOUR INNER STRENGTH                        153

Chapter 9:     Turning Your Adversity Into Opportunity              159

Chapter 10:    Finding Your Why                                     169

Chapter 11:    Surviving Your Dark Times                            183

Chapter 12:    Knowing Rejection Is Your Redirection                195

## SECTION 4:   ACHIEVING YOUR PERSONAL GROWTH                      207

Chapter 13:    Seeing Your True Colors                              213

Chapter 14:    Realizing Your Aspirations                           223

Chapter 15:    Perfecting Your Persistent Politeness                237

Chapter 16:   Connecting Within Your Six Degrees of Separation   251

**SECTION 5:   THRIVING IN YOUR TRUE PATH                        263**

Chapter 17:   Flowing With Your Life's Currents                 269

Chapter 18:   Embracing Your Regrets                            283

Chapter 19:   Harnessing Your Power of Aloha                    297

Chapter 20:   Manifesting Your Dreams                           311

Chapter 21:   Cultivating Your Winning Mindset—"It's On"        325

Chapter 22:   Your Daydreaming With Purpose                     339


A Final Note:   Living Aloha                                    351

About the Author                                               359

About the Author (in Hawaiian Pidgin Language)                 363

About Derick Sebastian's Music and Creative Offerings          369

About Derick Sebastian's Life Coaching                         373

Book Derick Sebastian as a Speaker or Keynote Performer         377

www.DerickSebastian.com

www.DerickSebastian.com

# CHARTING THE OCEAN OF DREAMS

by Michael A. Aczon

"Only those who will risk going too far
can possibly find out how far one can go."

— T. S. Eliot

**H**ave you ever wondered how a single idea can ripple through your life, transforming dreams into reality? The journey of turning daydreams into purpose-filled actions is a powerful one, and it's a journey Derick Sebastian has mastered. This book, *Daydreaming With Purpose*, is a testament to the magic that happens when dreams meet determination.

The Pacific Ocean is made up of countless individual drops of water. *Daydreaming With Purpose* is a reminder that when each of those individual drops of water is brought close together in the Aloha Spirit, they become an entire ocean that can be shared by people who live thousands of miles apart.

The first time I experienced Derick Sebastian was at a musical artist intensive at a college in the hills of Los Angeles. Based on my experience as an entertainment lawyer, I was invited to teach music business courses to eager, ambitious, and talented artists. I was seated in the theater during an artist showcase. On the stage stood a tall, handsome Hawaiian native man in front of an amplifier rig and holding an ukulele in his hands.

My initial reaction to seeing Derick poised to play for the audience was that he was going to serenade them with traditional Hawaiian songs, or he was a novelty act of some kind. I soon found out I was way off base. The moment Derick hit the first note on his ukulele, I was mesmerized by the combination of beauty, power, and virtuosity that was to come. One moment, Derick was lifting notes from the strings, sharing the joy he has experienced in his life; the next moment, it seemed like his fingers would press all the way through the neck of his ukulele as he exposed the pain and darkness he had experienced in his life.

Derick's amazing sharing of music was met by a standing ovation from an audience touched by his gift of song. That performance was the start of a very beautiful personal, professional, and spiritual relationship between Derick and me. During this time, I have witnessed him unfolding as a man, a father, an artist, and now as an author.

Throughout my career as a professional in the entertainment and art world, I have encountered hundreds—if not thousands—of artists, all of whom are dreamers of some kind wanting to share their gifts with others. Their shared trait of dreaming a dream and manifesting it into reality is what makes their art come to life, bringing joy to others and making the world a better place. If the world could be a better place filled with joy if everyone simply daydreamed and brought those daydreams to life, I began to ask myself,

"Why doesn't everyone do the same thing artists do with their daydreams?" This brought up an even more interesting question—why do some people not daydream at all?

I discovered through conversations with those who talked to me about their daydreaming that often when people daydream, it's to distract themselves from the task of exploring themselves and their respective paths. Some felt that daydreaming might lead to having to encounter a traumatic event in their past that they've been avoiding. Others have been advised by healthcare professionals that their daydreaming is a medical condition that can be fixed with prescription medication. Others dove into lifestyle patterns that proved to be harmful to themselves and those they love. While all of these behaviors are effective methods of self-preservation, they also potentially rob people of the possible joys that await them if they simply allow themselves to daydream and see where those daydreams will take them.

Successful people like Derick have instead found a way to explore their lives, allow themselves to daydream, embrace daydreaming, and redirect their daydreams in a positive way to grow into who they are meant to be. As I got to know Derick over the years, I learned that by using his ukulele as a tool, he was able to wander around, into, and through his daydreaming and organize his daydreams into beautiful expressions of self that he incorporates into every aspect of his life.

With this powerful book, you will learn what an amazing thing daydreams can be if you pay attention to them, understand them, and use them to create a synthesized life of your own. Derick has captured the secrets of daydreaming, organized them in a way that is easy to follow, and passed them on to you, the reader, to uncover the power you have inside to become a virtuoso of your own daydreams.

Derick passes on to you the information and spirit he learned from his teachers, coupled with what he learned from his experiences. He guides you through how he has taken a journey through life complete with concrete steps to explore the enormity of life presented by your daydreams, followed by organizing them so your day-by-day actions can take you closer to making those dreams your reality. From the description of manifesting one of his own dreams in the initial chapter "Being Ready for Your Go Time" through his sign-off in the chapter "Your Daydreaming With Purpose," it's almost as if Derick is lovingly teaching you how to play a song written just for you on the ukulele just like he does.

When you follow the formulas and strategies in this book, you will discover so many things about yourself that can be applied immediately to manifest your dreams. Through your own exploration of your core beliefs and values using the questions posed in each chapter, you will better understand who you are and why you dream the dreams you dream. Derick then guides you through exercises and tips for acquiring the specific knowledge and skills needed to create a life that embraces the Power of Aloha, which is in every human.

Throughout this book, you will learn you are the key force in manifesting your daydreams. Allow Derick Sebastian to be your guide, taking you through chapters like "Finding Your Home," "Surviving Your Dark Times," and "Perfecting Your Persistent Politeness" to bring out the key force in you that can take your seemingly impossible dreams and live them out day-to-day. In the time I've known Derick, his inspiring sharing of his spirit and my implementing his guidance has brought me so much of the joy in my own life.

At this very moment, I am back at the college on the Los Angeles hilltop— the very spot where I met Derick Sebastian twenty years ago—sharing the experiences, knowledge, and sum total of the dreams I had over a half-century ago about building a life and finding a career that would allow me to be surrounded by individuals who have the courage to pursue their aspirations, bring them to fruition, and share their achievements with the world.

Looking east, I see the sun rising to bring about another day I can live out my own dream. Looking west, I see the Pacific Ocean. In doing so, I can feel the amazing connection I have with Derick Sebastian who—while physically miles and miles away from me in Maui—is right next to me. By embracing our individual dreams and sharing those dreams with each other and everyone we come in contact with every day, the two of us have integrated our lives in the way all of those drops of water in the Pacific Ocean are connected, so we are one with each other and with the universe.

I invite you to do the same. Get ready for an amazing ride into the joys of your own daydreams. You will find that by embracing what you learn in *Daydreaming With Purpose*, you will be able to travel on your own power across the ocean of challenges to the shore where your daydream can begin.

Michael A. Aczon
Entertainment Lawyer, Artist Manager,
Author, Educator, *Ohana*
www.aczon.org

www.DerickSebastian.com

# YOUR ALOHA AWAKENING

"Twenty years from now you will be more disappointed by the things that you didn't do than by the ones you did do."

— H. Jackson Brown, Jr.

Y ou know deep down in your heart you're meant to do something bigger and better on this earth, but perhaps you find yourself too afraid to try or even think about "What if?" What are your daydreams that warm your soul? If your entire life you've been listening to everybody else's opinions, doing what they say, becoming who they think you should be, this path is leading you to an incomplete, unfulfilled, and ultimately boring life of mediocrity. You may be frustrated, unsure, unmotivated, and angry because you feel you're wasting precious time and not living out your life's purpose.

Are you waking up every day and asking yourself, "What am I doing?" or "Who am I?" Are you just going through the motions daily, feeling unmotivated? Are you tired of going to school and studying something to be something you don't want to be? Are you completely over your job, working hard for others in a role that means nothing to you? Do you have big dreams and exciting ideas, but they are always shot down by that inner voice, echoing the doubts and criticisms of loved ones or close friends, that says, "You're not good enough," "I think you should do this or be that," "Your dreams are unrealistic," or "You can't do this…. You can't do that!"

You know it's time to make a change, but you find yourself standing on the edge, not knowing what's on the other side. You're afraid to take that leap of faith. You're thinking, "Should I try?" "What if I fail?" "What if they were right about me?" or "Will I be letting down my loved ones and close friends if I don't succeed?"

I understand your pain, frustration, and confusion. I've been there too, feeling the weight of doubt and living an unfulfilled life for others instead of myself. I know what it's like to hear others speak negatively about your dreams.

In this book, you will learn how to be true to yourself, tune out the noise, and follow your heart. This book is more than just a collection of my stories. It is an exploration of the relentless pursuit of dreams, the power of perseverance, and the magic that happens when preparation meets opportunity. Each chapter delves into a different aspect of the journey, from my thrilling experiences performing around the world and at major sporting events and developing heartfelt relationships to the quiet, reflective moments of daydreaming with purpose. Along the way, I'll share the lessons I've learned, tell you about the people who have inspired me, and reveal my biggest daydreams and the faith that has sustained me.

If you apply the wisdom, knowledge, experience, skills, strategies, and techniques offered in this book to your life, you will achieve the true meaning of "Daydreaming With Purpose."

I haven't been through everything, but I've been through a lot. I don't have all the answers because I am still learning in my journey through life. However, I believe that through my trials, tribulations, failures, and successes, you can learn and become a better person with an open, fulfilling perspective moving forward.

Daydreaming with purpose is scary, and it will take a lot of courage, especially if you continue taking steps forward and relentlessly pursuing your goals despite your current situation. You will feel that impostor syndrome, the urge to give up, and perhaps try to convince yourself that maybe your dreams aren't for you. But I want you to know it's okay to be human and feel that way. Embrace it, but don't hold on to it. It's important to realize you're simply growing and developing your character. It's okay to rest, but it's not okay to give up. You need to keep on keeping on because everything leads to something. Realize that you are bigger and stronger than you think. You're a gift to this world; you're a miracle.

At the heart of this journey lies the true essence of Aloha. In Hawaiian culture, Aloha is more than a greeting—it's a way of life. Aloha means love, peace, compassion, and having mutual respect. It's the breath of life, the spirit that connects us all. It's about living with an open heart, embracing each moment with gratitude, and spreading kindness wherever you go. As you embark on this journey of self-discovery and transformation, remember to carry the Spirit of Aloha with you. Let it guide your actions, inspire your dreams, and remind you of the interconnectedness of all life.

With Aloha in your heart, there's no limit to what you can achieve. Now is the time for your Aloha Awakening.

I am here to be your virtual mentor, your accountability partner. I want to be the shoulder you can lean on during tough times. I want to be your friend, the person and resource you look to in overcoming your challenges.

Are you ready to step outside of your box? Are you ready to expand your comfort zone and step into the new person you are becoming? Are you ready to achieve your goals? If so, great! Let's get started and make this journey together! Now is your time.

Let's go!

Derick Sebastian

www.DerickSebastian.com

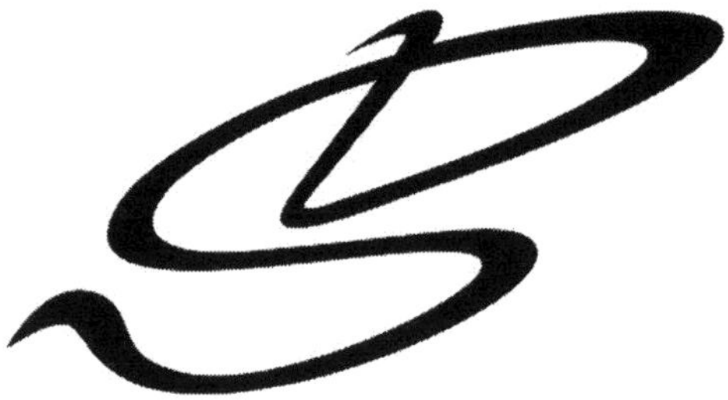

# SECTION 1:

# PREPARING FOR YOUR JOURNEY

"The journey of a thousand miles begins with a single step."

— Lao Tzu

# DOWNLOAD AND STREAM SONG FOR FREE!

www.DerickSebastian.com/BestDay

# BEST DAY

## Song Written and Performed by Derick Sebastian

I've got this feeling
A good, good feeling
It's the best day of my life

I've got sunshine in my pocket
I feel good, good hearted
It's the best day because I'm alive

I'll jump and touch the sky
Living life full day and night
This is the best day of my life

I got rainbows all around me
These colors set me free
It's the best day of my life

I'll spread my wings and fly
Oh so high
It's the best day because I'm alive

I will fall but I know I'll stand

I won't give up 'cause I've got your helping hand

I'm singing oh

www.DerickSebastian.com

www.DerickSebastian.com

# CHAPTER 1

# BEING READY FOR YOUR "GO TIME"

"Opportunities don't happen. You create them."

— Chris Grosser

**W**hen your daydream becomes reality, will you be ready? Are you fully prepared to step into your destiny when your big opportunity arrives?

**MY STORY**

It was a cool, crisp night on March 10, 2016, in the heart of downtown Los Angeles as I walked through the vibrant scene. The atmosphere was unlike anything on my home island of Maui. People filled the streets in every direction as if this were the only place in the city that was alive. Gatherings were everywhere, with the surround-sound of endless chatter, bursts of laughter, and occasional screams of excitement. It was a party, a celebration—it was LA! I continued walking, eyes wide open, taking it all in, and then, bam! There it was—the astonishing Staples Center, home of the Los Angeles Lakers!

I was nervous beyond what I could ever imagine. As I walked toward the VIP entrance, I could feel the energy. I couldn't help noticing the towering statues of Elgin Baylor, Kareem Abdul-Jabbar, Magic Johnson, Jerry West, and Chick Hearn. Die-hard Lakers fans swarmed the arena, eagerly waiting to get in. It was a tidal wave of purple and gold. Working my way through several security checkpoints and then being guided through some executive hallways and back tunnels, I found myself at center court doing a sound check with my ukulele. I was at a loss for words and felt six feet small. The place was huge. Seats everywhere, lights flashing, music bumping—the energy was electrifying.

Oh, and all the NBA players were warming up right next to me. Cheerleaders were running through routines. Sports anchors and media were everywhere. It was completely surreal.

After the sound check and a few practice runs (everything sounded amazing), I couldn't help looking up and staring at the huge, state-of-the-art, center-hung video LIVE 4HD scoreboard above me, complete with a booming sound system I could feel right through my body.

"Derick. Hey, Derick! Are you good?" asked the game operations director.

"Yes, I'm good," I quickly answered, snapping back to reality. It was time to get off the court, and I was led through another set of secret tunnels and finally reached my green room. I sat down, pinched myself a few times, took a few deep breaths, and tried my very best to be present in the moment, knowing in a short while I would be performing the national anthem on the biggest stage I'd ever been on. I sensed my daydream manifesting—my life was about to change.

I got dressed, did my stretches, breathing, and surely said some prayers. I wired up my in-ear monitors and tuned my Kanile'a ukulele. I was ready to go.

The doors suddenly swung open—it was my game operations contact.

"All right, Derick, you ready? We have about twenty-four minutes to showtime. It's go time!"

I took another deep breath, but I felt I just couldn't get enough air. As we left the green room walking toward the players' tunnel, I was absolutely shocked to see video cameras following me out; endless photographers were all lined up against the wall, sounding clicks after clicks and triggering flash after flash. *I guess this is part of it all*, I thought. I have no credentials for this.

I was guided by several large-bodied security guards, and as we entered the players' tunnel, the crowd noise got louder and louder—and even louder. It was a completely packed house!

The music was pumping like the beat of my heart. The energy was overwhelming, and there I was, walking along courtside, getting into position. I was in awe of what was around me. I saw celebrities everywhere, sitting in every courtside seat available. People were screaming and yelling to get the players' attention. And there was LeBron James of the Cleveland

Cavaliers, and yes, Kobe Bryant of the LA Lakers, getting ready for the big game. It was a sellout crowd of 20,000-plus fans—it was completely insane!

"All right, Derick, we are three minutes out. Please start walking to your position at center court!" said my game operations person. The countdown began in my in-ear monitors, "Derick, you got thirty seconds, ten seconds, five, four, three, two, one!" Suddenly, the lights went out completely, except one big spotlight, shining directly on me.

That's when I realized this moment was real. I was standing center court in Staples Center with thousands of people just staring at me. I was beyond nervous. My hands were sweating, and I could hear my heartbeat pounding out of my chest.

Suddenly, that God-like deep voice of the Lakers' legendary longtime public announcer, Lawrence Tanter, came on and said, "Ladies and gentlemen, please remove your hats for the playing of our national anthem, this evening by Maui's very own Derick Sebastian!"

It was finally happening. I took another deep breath, said another quick prayer, and I went for it!

I played the first note, then the second, and "The Star-Spangled Banner" just started to flow and sing through my ukulele. To my surprise, I heard someone shout out the Polynesian celebratory call, "Chee Hoo!" A few times during my performance, the crowd started to roar, and it completely drowned out my in-ear monitors—I couldn't hear a thing, not even my ukulele. Deep down inside, I seriously panicked, praying and concentrating the best I could to stay on course and timing with the song. I'm not sure how I really did it, but I blocked out everything around me and was laser-focused on every single note I had to hit throughout the song.

Before I knew it, I was playing my final notes, strumming as fast as I could, building up to the last hard strum, but again, the crowd beat me to it. The entire place was roaring, cheering, and clapping!

After my hard ending strum, I emoted a big yell, pointing up to the sky, giving thanks and praise to God, and just started crying. I had so many emotions I had to control, especially keeping focus and composure. I finally let it all out and felt I could finally breathe. The weight was off my shoulders, and I just couldn't believe how loud the crowd's noise and applause was. I felt this energy through my bones. It was done. I finally did it—mission accomplished. I was escorted off the court while fans gave me high-fives and praise.

I finally got back to the green room, sat down, and tried to process what exactly had just happened. The room was quiet—I mean really quiet; I could probably hear a pin drop. I could even hear my heart still pounding in my chest. I had just started putting my ukulele away and wrapping up my equipment when my phone rang—and it kept on ringing, and ringing, non-stop.

The unexpected circus had begun. I spent the entire post-performance doing phone interviews with local news from Los Angeles and Hawaii. Apparently, without even knowing, video clips of my performance were going viral on social media. My phone was overwhelmed by calls, texts, and notifications. I finally had to turn it off for a little while so I could come up for some air. And, of course, I had to save some battery to speak to my wife and boys.

Unfortunately, I didn't even get to sit down and watch the game, which I was totally looking forward to because it was my first time ever attending a regular season NBA game. But I was overcome by the unexpected media madness around me—it was crazy!

The game was finally over, and it seemed my adventurous night was finally coming to an end. My support team and I decided to go out for a quick bite to conclude the evening, but I was about to experience one of the craziest pieces of news ever.

During dinner, I got a one-word text from a dear friend, Patrick Ewing, Jr., simply reading, "*SportsCenter*!" I had no idea what he was talking about.

Then, shortly after we got to our hotel, my wife Raymi called and asked, "Are you seeing what's going on in social media?"

"No. I've been taking a break from my phone."

"I think you better get to the closest TV and turn on ESPN."

We rushed up to my room, turned on ESPN, and waited. Just a few minutes in, there I was—and Hawaii-icon sports anchor Neil Everett and co-host Stan Verrett were talking about me. I was featured in a thirty-second clip on ESPN's *SportsCenter*, playing the national anthem on my very own ukulele. I just couldn't believe it. I was completely numb. I had no words to describe the feeling. Oh my God! Wow! My daydream had become my reality.

Being on ESPN's *SportsCenter* was the ultimate cherry-on-top ending. Growing up, I had the wildest fantasy about being on *SportsCenter*, and now it had happened completely unexpectedly. It was surreal and beyond what I could ever imagine—it was insane, like seriously, beyond insane.

Performing for the Lakers in LA was a daydream that took seven years to become reality, but my dream had finally come true. On March 10, 2016, I made history by becoming the first-ever ukulele player to perform the national anthem for the LA Lakers on their home court at Staples Center. It was a night to remember because it was also Kobe Bryant and LeBron James' final square-off before Bryant's retirement.

I would give many national anthem performances in the years to come, and thanks to my many, many years of practice, I was ready for go time.

## WHAT I LEARNED

I realized in that moment my life had changed forever. I learned no matter how big or small your dreams are, they do come true. Even if your dreams seem to be completely out of this world, as long as you keep believing your vision is non-negotiable, you will achieve your exact vision. The truth is, impossible really means, "I'm possible." The biggest, most important lesson I learned was to never give up and always believe in yourself.

## EXERCISE

1.  Clarifying Your Vision

    - Question: What is your daydream? What is your vision? Don't limit your imagination—what do you ultimately see yourself doing?

    - Activity: Create a vision board to visually represent your dream or vision.

- Reflection: How does seeing your dreams visually add motivation and clarity?

_____

_____

_____

_____

_____

_____

_____

_____

_____

_____

2. Reflecting on Your Passion

- Question: Think about a moment when you felt a strong nudge toward pursuing something you're passionate about. What dream or aspiration have you hesitated to pursue because it felt too uncomfortable or challenging?

- Activity: Write a detailed journal entry about this aspiration and break down the dream into smaller, manageable steps to create a detailed action plan.

- Reflection: How do you feel as you outline your action plan? How can the qualities and skills you already have be applied to pursuing your current dreams? How do you plan to overcome any fears or doubts that may surface?

_____

_____

_____

_____

_____

_____

_____

_____

_____

_____

3.  Listening to Your Inner Voice

- Question: When was the last time you listened to your inner voice and followed a path that felt right? What small, achievable goal can you set today to help align yourself with your bigger dreams?

- Activity: Spend ten to fifteen minutes in a quiet place, practicing mindfulness meditation focused on listening to your inner voice. Then, set the above goal and visualize yourself achieving it in vivid detail every day until you do.

- Reflection: Write down any insights or messages your inner voice communicated. Keep a daily log of your visualization sessions—how does this practice influence your motivation and mindset?

_____

_____

_____

_____

_____

_____

_____

_____

_____

_____

_____

4. Prioritizing Your Dreams

- Question: How can you rearrange your daily routine to prioritize actions that bring you closer to your dreams?

- Activity: Conduct an audit of your daily routine and identify activities that do not contribute to your goals. Create a commitment statement outlining how you will implement the necessary changes.

- Reflection: Analyze your audit and reflect on the effect these changes have on your progress toward your dreams.

_____

_____

_____

_____

_____

_____

_____

## FIVE TIPS FOR BEING READY FOR YOUR "GO TIME"

1. **Be Open to Your Life's Nudges:** Life often nudges us toward our passions and daydreams. Pay attention to those moments of inspiration and embrace them wholeheartedly.

2. **Embrace Your Discomfort:** Dreams should push you out of your comfort zone. If your dream doesn't make you uncomfortable, it might not be big enough. Embrace the discomfort as a sign that you're aiming for something meaningful.

3. **Follow Your Inner Calling:** Listen to what your heart truly desires. Your daydreams are often reflections of your deepest desires and talents. Trust that what you're seeking is also seeking you.

4. **Set Realistic Goals:** Break your dreams down into smaller, achievable goals. Each step you take brings you closer to realizing your ultimate vision. Set realistic milestones and celebrate your progress along the way.

5. **Prioritize Your Dreams:** Make your dreams a priority. Whether it's dedicating time to practice, networking with like-minded individuals, or seeking opportunities, prioritize actions that align with your dreams.

## SUMMARY

Performing the national anthem for the Lakers at the Staples Center was a dream come true, the result of years of relentless practice and unwavering determination. This performance was just the beginning. It opened the door to dozens of opportunities. Each performance was a testament to the countless hours I dedicated to my craft. I suspect I put in far more than 10,000 hours of practice. It's impossible to know the exact number, but what matters is when it was "go time," I was ready. I crushed it, and my career has grown exponentially because I was prepared.

However, preparation alone isn't enough. The journey to achieving our dreams often begins with finding our true home, a place where we feel rooted and supported. In this book, we'll explore how the search for a sense of belonging shapes our path.

## CALL TO ACTION

I challenge you to commit to practicing and working toward mastering your craft every day. Approach your daydreams with relentless determination and dedicate yourself fully to pursuing your passion. This consistent effort will prepare you for the opportunities that lie ahead. When your "go time" arrives—when that defining moment comes—you'll be ready to seize it with confidence. This is your chance not just to participate, but to excel, stand out, and become one of the best in the world at what you love doing. Remember, greatness isn't achieved overnight; it's built through daily dedication and an unwavering belief in your potential.

www.DerickSebastian.com

# CHAPTER 2

# FINDING YOUR HOME

"Life is filled with unanswered questions, but it is the courage to seek those answers that continues to give meaning to life."

— J. D. Stroube

Where is your home? Where do you go to find strength? Which people in your life have become your home?

**MY STORY**

I was born in Maui in 1982, and growing up there, I had a very interesting childhood. I had really bad asthma and eczema, and I was always sick. I was the youngest of four siblings (Rose, Roger, Debra, and me), and they basically gave me everything I wanted because I was the baby of the family. My mother was a stay-at-home mom. My dad was a quiet but hardworking man. He worked at a historic sugarcane processing plant on Maui where he was a lead mechanic responsible for fixing all the big machinery, especially the "crusher," a gigantic machine that crushed and compressed all the sugarcane plants.

When I was an innocent little boy, I looked forward to seeing my dad, Rogelio, every night. My memories of him are very vague, but I remember a few things like always going to a super-cool toy store in Kahului where he would spoil me by buying all the toys I wanted. I remember sitting on my dad's lap, bouncing up and down as if I were riding a rodeo bull. My dad wouldn't say much, but he always gave a little smile, which was his ultimate way of showing his love.

Then, one night when I was three, my mom got a late evening call. All I heard were screams and cries. She could barely say a word. My siblings and I were so scared; we just sat there as Mom sobbed, gasping for air with every breath.

When she could, Mom told us Dad had been involved in a horrible industrial accident. He was laying between the two platforms of the "crusher" when someone accidentally pressed the operating button. It was not a fast death. It was horrifically unimaginable. We were shocked. We couldn't believe it. Dad was gone at just forty-two.

At the time, I didn't really understand what was going on. All I knew was so many family members, friends, and everyone in between were coming over every day and night to check on us. Everyone was sad and crying. Mom just kept telling me, "Dad is going to be sleeping for a long time."

By kindergarten, Dad's passing didn't really affect me, but as I got older, an odd feeling started to creep up on me. At open houses, school meetings, functions, and fundraisers, I saw all my classmates' parents, siblings, family members, and friends attending, but most of the time it was just me with my older sister because Mom was too busy juggling several jobs to make ends meet.

I didn't do much after school. My life was boring. I went to school, came home, watched cartoons, played a little, and before I knew it, it was time for bed—and I did the same thing over and over again for years.

Then I started asking, "Why me? Why don't I have my dad? Why did my dad have to die so early?" My sisters and brother were great company, and we had a lot of fun. I also had some awesome neighborhood friends, but still, I felt the loneliness and void of my father's absence. I started feeling empty and confused. A silent bitterness weighed me down every day.

Around age nine, despite my asthma, I was finally allowed to play baseball. I was surprised because Mom was so protective and tried not to let me out of her sight. I was always sick, and maybe she was scared of losing me too. Nonetheless, playing baseball was an absolute high. It was like I was born again. I really enjoyed it, and it sort of felt like I had found my way, truly filling the void of not having a dad.

But despite the happiness I found playing baseball, it slowly began to suck because my family missed most of my games. Mom was always busy working, and even Rose, Roger, and Debra couldn't make my games because they were busy with their own school and sporting activities. I understood our family was busy, but still, it really sucked. Baseball was the "something" that gave me the opportunity to be excited, look forward to something, and make my family proud, but my family members only came to my games a few times.

It was a strange and difficult time. I felt baseball gave me something exciting to look forward to, but at the same time, I felt alone. And this aloneness led to a little internal spiral where I sought more attention.

Growing up without my dad made me somewhat insecure. I was a big and tall grade schooler, so it wasn't hard for me to put up a front. I wasn't necessarily a bully, but I was surely a presence.

I truly believe I was actually a nice kid—at least that's what I felt—but because I felt I needed to be seen and heard, I started to hang around with some friends who weren't the best influence.

In fifth grade, we had an event called "DARE Day," which stands for Drug Abuse Resistance Education. It was an island-wide, super-cool event where all the fifth graders from every school gathered for the entire day. We watched Maui County first responders perform a ton of demonstrations and presentations. A helicopter did several flyovers. We even had a monster truck smashing cars. It was awesome!

That day, I was with my friends in a pretty big group when we ran into a group of boys from another school who didn't like us. That is when my life changed.

I honestly didn't do anything except stand there and "cruise with the boys," but for some reason, the other group of boys came directly after me. I got pushed, punched, choked, and thrown to the ground. I was outnumbered, and none of my so-called friends stepped in to help. I was surprised. I didn't know what to think or do. I couldn't fight back—it was like six to one.

After, all I remember is tons of police breaking up the fight. I was escorted to a police car, which brought me back to my school. I sat in the principal's office where I was asked question after question, but I didn't know what to say except, "I was just hanging around with my friends, and then all of a sudden, I was being mobbed." I didn't know who the other kids were or what school they came from, nothing. I was just with the wrong people, at the wrong place, at the wrong time.

Looking back, even at ten, I knew I was heading in the wrong direction, and that brawl was a life lesson learned. I needed to change my friends and, more importantly, change my thinking. I realized the people I hung around reflected who I was going to become.

Finding your home isn't just about the physical space you occupy; it's about finding a sense of belonging and purpose. Through the ups and downs, the feelings of loneliness and moments of connection, I discovered home is where you feel accepted, supported, and truly yourself.

**WHAT I LEARNED**

My childhood struggles were not obstacles but steppingstones that prepared me for life's journey. The questions, doubts, and moments of loneliness weren't setbacks; they were essential experiences that shaped my perspective and developed my true character. I came to realize these early challenges weren't happening to me, but for me, guiding me toward growth and resilience. I learned to perform even without my family present, and you become the sum of the five people you spend the most time with. Being alone pushed me to look deeper within myself, making me stronger. Most importantly, being unable to play many sports freed up time to learn to play the ukulele.

**EXERCISE**

1. Reflecting on Childhood and Identity

   - Question: How was your childhood? Was it loving and supportive or tough and unstable? How did your family shape who you are today?

   - Activity: Create a family tree. Note significant stories or memories with each family member. Then write a letter to your younger self.

   - Reflection: How do these family connections and reflections on your experiences influence your sense of identity and belonging?

   _____

   _____

   _____

   _____

   _____

   _____

2. Exploring Key Childhood Memories

   - Question: Can you recall a specific, standout moment with your family? How did that moment shape your understanding of love and connection?

- Activity: Take a mindful memory walk or visualize that moment. Then write about the event from the perspective of each family member involved.

- Reflection: How does this exercise affect your understanding of your past and others' perspectives?

_____

_____

_____

_____

_____

_____

_____

_____

_____

3. Understanding and Reframing Childhood Experiences

    - Question: How can you practice compassion and kindness toward yourself when reflecting on challenging childhood memories?

    - How does looking at yourself from your parents or guardians' perspective during a challenging moment change your perception of that event?

- Activity: Practice a guided self-compassion meditation. Then write about the event from the perspective of each family member involved.

- Reflection: How do these exercises help you reframe and better understand your experiences?

_____

_____

_____

_____

_____

_____

_____

_____

_____

_____

4. Applying Childhood Lessons to Your Present

- Question: Reflect on the lessons you learned from childhood experiences. How can those lessons inform and guide you as you move forward?

- Activity: Identify and list the core values you developed from your childhood experiences.

- Reflection: How do these values guide your decisions and actions today?

_____

_____

_____

_____

_____

_____

## FIVE TIPS FOR FINDING YOUR HOME

1. **Realize You Had No Control Over What You Were Born Into:** We all come from different walks of life. Reflect and write down your own childhood experiences and the role of family members in shaping you.

2. **Accept Your Parents or Guardians Raised You the Best They Knew How at That Moment:** Draw a memorable moment with your family, being open to exploring and connecting emotionally with your own story.

3. **Remember, Through the Ups and Downs, You Were Loved in Many Different Ways:** Imagine yourself in your parents or guardians' shoes during your childhood. Write about how you would feel and react to raising a child like yourself.

4. **Practice Self-Compassion:** The struggle is real, but it's not permanent. Accept your emotions, good or bad. Practice compassion and kindness toward yourself as you navigate these feelings.

5. **Reflect on What You've Learned:** Your childhood shapes your perspective on life. Reflect on the lessons you can learn from those early experiences and how they can influence your future. Be grateful for the things that didn't work out in your youth because they made room for even better opportunities to come your way later.

## SUMMARY

I had to grow up fast. It surely wasn't perfect, but one great thing it did was build my character. It gave me a bit of perspective and appreciation for life. I didn't take things for granted. Even though my family didn't have much, it felt like we had everything because we had each other, a loving family. When life gets tough, we'll have questions and doubts. We have to go through them whether we like it or not. We may not understand the "why" of any given moment, but later, we'll eventually find answers to help make sense of it all. Childhood is our life's foundation, and it plays a huge role as we grow older. Be grateful for your childhood because it is the reason you are who you are today. While finding my home provided the stability I needed, life's greatest blessings often come disguised as challenges. As I navigated my early years, I discovered adversity could lead to the most unexpected and profound blessings. Join me as we continue to uncover these hidden gifts together.

## CALL TO ACTION

Reflect on your childhood and see what life was teaching you all along. I challenge you to always remember life doesn't happen to you; it happens for you. I challenge you to always remember that even when you lose loved ones (parents, friends, etc.), their souls will always be with you to guide your path home, even if only in loving memories. In Hawaii, because we are so far removed from the rest of the world, we often find "home" in our friends. So, your home and family may be found in those you love who may not be your blood. For this, too, is the Aloha Spirit in action.

www.DerickSebastian.com

# CHAPTER 3

# UNCOVERING YOUR HIDDEN BLESSINGS

"What seems to us as bitter trials are often blessings in disguise."

— Oscar Wilde

**A**s you look back on your life, what hidden blessings have emerged to mentor, guide, and show you the way? Who are the people, not related by blood, who showed up in your life and helped lead you on your path?

## MY STORY

I was entering sixth grade, transitioning to middle school at Maui Waena Intermediate. I was nervous, a little scared. I was coming off that crazy fight in fifth grade, and I had to change who I was hanging around with. I surely didn't want that to happen again; I was scared.

Nevertheless, it was a new school, new faces, a new beginning. I was looking forward to making new friends, playing baseball, and just growing up—not being so much the "baby" in the family, and, of course, trying to fill the void of being fatherless.

But I guess God (or the Universe) had other plans for me. Just a few months into my first year in middle school, something went wrong, and I started to get really sick. I couldn't breathe properly and experienced frequent shortness of breath. My asthma got so bad that my doctors said I had to take a break from sports and any activities that strained my respiratory system. Baseball came to a sudden halt. I was devastated. I felt like I was back to square one—feeling down, just going to school, coming straight home, watching cartoons, just being plain bored. This time around, it really sucked. It felt like my world had come crashing down.

It wasn't long before things shifted again. It was a normal day at school. I was just going through the motions. Then one day when the morning recess bell rang, to my surprise, I saw our school security guard, Mr. Sam Ellis—who was already a longtime family friend—sitting on a bench playing his ukulele. His music felt so good that it was as if my soul were dancing inside me. A few students had gathered around him, and they were having a great time—talking, laughing, and simply enjoying each other's company. Mr. Ellis kept singing and smiling, and for the first time in my life, I felt pure joy. Not having a father and feeling bored after school, I saw in Mr. Ellis a smile, a light, and a love that reminded me of my dad.

That day changed my life.

Mr. Ellis invited me over to sit with him on the bench while he strummed away on his fascinating instrument. I was mesmerized. I completely locked in on his rhythm and how fluid he was while singing and playing his ukulele. Mr. Ellis was having fun and laughing up a storm while making up his own lyrics on the fly—it was so cool.

All of a sudden, he said, "Here. You try play."

I was so surprised he allowed me to play. I truly did not know what to do except strum a few times, which did not sound good, but I immediately knew this was the start of something great.

I got so excited, and I wanted to be part of the energy Mr. Ellis was giving off. From then on, every day at school, I made it a point to go watch Mr. Ellis play his ukulele. Going to school had become exciting again.

Mr. Ellis and I ended up meeting on that same bench every morning and lunch recess just to play ukulele. It was so much fun—like a breath of fresh air every single time. Playing the ukulele with Mr. Ellis took all the worries and stress about my asthma away—especially the part where I couldn't play baseball. I was carefree and just having fun, like truly fulfilling fun. This time with him gave me hope for a better future.

The only problem was I didn't have an ukulele to practice on at home. When all the stars align, you have to believe God is looking out for you and bring about what is best for you.

One day, my older brother Roger came home from school, and to my surprise, he was holding an ukulele. I asked, "What's this?" He said, "Oh, it's from my ukulele ensemble class." I just couldn't believe it—it was like an answer from God—the ukulele just fell from the sky.

Roger practiced on his ukulele, but when he was done, I immediately took it to practice on. I practiced way more than he did. Eventually, the drill became that he brought his school ukulele home every day so I could practice. How it all panned out was the craziest thing. Access to my brother's ukulele was a blessing.

Around the same time, my uncle Eddie, who also had an ukulele, offered to let me borrow his when I didn't have one. It was so fun—we had lots of jam sessions at home.

It felt like the stars had aligned perfectly!

Then I stumbled upon my neighbor down the street, Melvin. I knew who he was but never really spoke to him. Well, he played the ukulele too, but on a completely different level. He was strumming all kinds of styles, picking all kinds of techniques—it was absolutely mind-blowing. I was mesmerized and totally shocked by how he made his ukulele sound like a slack key guitar with a hint of rock 'n' roll. I was one of the lucky ones he took under his wing to teach his sophisticated style of playing. I learned different strumming and picking techniques, scales, runs, chord progressions, and songs above and beyond my belief. I was eleven and becoming a musician.

Melvin played a huge role in me learning the ukulele—I wanted to play like Melvin. He inspired me to learn different strumming and picking styles. Some events motivate you to step out of your comfort circle, and Melvin was just that. He was kind enough to show and teach me complex techniques on the ukulele.

I practiced, practiced, and practiced—day and night. And life felt good again, just like when I had gone to the toy store with my dad as a three-year-old.

I practiced like crazy, at least five hours a day, every day for three years. I woke up before 6 a.m. so I could practice ukulele an hour before going to school. I played ukulele with Mr. Ellis at school. Then after school, I practiced another couple of hours. Then I did my homework, had dinner, and practiced again in the evening.

I practiced so much my fingertips on my left hand bled, but I kept going. Over time, my fingers developed calluses that covered the cuts and became stronger.

Mom took me to the local music stores to buy ukulele music cassette tapes. I played them over and over. It sounded like a broken record—play, rewind, play, rewind, play, rewind. I practiced obsessively, and it drove my household insane.

I kept this practice ritual for the three years I was at Maui Waena Intermediate School. I totaled nearly 5,500 hours of practice. I continued practicing relentlessly, and by the time I was a junior in high school, I had already practiced well over 10,000 hours.

It took me just six years to hit 10,000 hours of practice—the 10,000-hour goal popularized by Malcolm Gladwell's book *Outliers*. Gladwell proposed it takes 10,000 hours of intensive practice to achieve mastery of complex skills. This principle has been applied to musicians, athletes, and artists, emphasizing the immense dedication required to reach the top of any field. For me, those 10,000 hours spent relentlessly honing my skills on the ukulele were driven by a passion that kept me practicing day and night. It was a journey of perseverance, where every strum, every note, and every chord brought me closer to mastering the instrument that had become my lifeline, my love, my joy, and my daydream.

Was I a master on the ukulele in just six years of playing? I didn't think so. But I knew I had a passion for the instrument that had saved my life. Finding the ukulele truly uncovered my hidden blessing!

## WHAT I LEARNED

My struggle with asthma, initially a seemingly devastating setback, unexpectedly became the gateway to discovering my passion for the ukulele. What started as a difficult and disheartening time transformed into the beginning of a joyful musical journey. The ukulele brought me hope, excitement, and curiosity, giving me a new reason to look forward to each day. This experience taught me that life's greatest challenges often lead to our most profound blessings, revealing hidden opportunities and igniting passions we might never have discovered otherwise. I also learned that mentors beyond my dad could guide me, helping me find purpose and giving me permission to dream. Mr. Ellis and Melvin both showed me how to live out my newfound passion.

## EXERCISE

1.  Identifying Hidden Blessings

    - Question: Think of something that happened that was a hidden blessing. Can you recall a time when a challenge or setback ultimately led to an unexpected opportunity or positive outcome?

    - Activity: Start a gratitude journal focused on hidden blessings and create a timeline of significant challenges with their positive outcomes.

- Reflection: How does focusing on hidden blessings change your perspective on current challenges, and how have these challenges shaped who you are today?

_____

_____

_____

_____

2. Growth Through Adversity

- Question: Reflect on a time when you faced a challenge that pushed you out of your comfort zone. How did that experience strengthen your resilience and prepare you for future challenges?

- Activity: Practice mindfulness meditation focused on recognizing hidden blessings. Write down insights about how adversity has influenced your resilience.

- Reflection: How does this exercise help you reframe your view of challenges and appreciate their positive aspects?

_____

_____

_____

_____

3. Clarifying Values and Priorities

- Question: Name some priorities or values that become clearer as a result of overcoming challenges. How has facing adversity influenced how you empathize with and support others?

- Activity: Write a letter to a specific challenge expressing gratitude for the lessons learned. Then, interview a mentor about the hidden blessings they discovered in their challenges.

- Reflection: How does this exercise help reframe your view of the challenge, and how do your mentor's stories resonate with your own experiences?

_____

_____

_____

_____

4. Visualizing Challenges and Opportunities

- Question: Think about a difficult situation you've overcome. How did that experience prepare you for future challenges?

- Activity: Create a vision board that includes both your goals and potential challenges. Write down insights about how visualizing both challenges and blessings affects your motivation and mindset.

- Reflection: How has this activity influenced your perspective on current and future challenges?

_____

_____

_____

_____

## FIVE TIPS FOR UNCOVERING YOUR HIDDEN BLESSINGS

1. **Opportunity for Growth:** Trials can push you out of your comfort zone and challenge you to develop new skills, perspectives, and strengths. Embrace these challenges as opportunities for personal growth, leading to profound self-improvement and resilience.

2. **Clarify Priorities:** Facing trials can help you reassess your priorities and values, gaining clarity on what truly matters to you. Focus on the essentials, letting go of distractions or superficial pursuits, and direct your energy toward what brings genuine fulfillment and happiness.

3. **Strengthen Resilience:** Enduring trials builds resilience, the ability to bounce back from setbacks and adversity. Each challenge you overcome strengthens your resilience muscles, preparing you to face future obstacles with greater confidence and determination.

4. **Deepen Empathy and Compassion:** Going through difficult times cultivates empathy and compassion toward others who may be

experiencing similar struggles. It fosters a deeper understanding of human suffering and a desire to support and uplift those in need. This experience will strengthen your connections with others and foster a sense of community.

5. **Open Doors to Unexpected Opportunities:** Sometimes trials lead you down unexpected paths or present opportunities you wouldn't have encountered otherwise. Embrace these challenges with an open mind; they can lead to new friendships, experiences, or paths that ultimately enrich your life in ways you couldn't have imagined.

## SUMMARY

It's often difficult to see the blessings in the moment. My journey with Mr. Ellis and the ukulele taught me even the most challenging circumstances can lead to unexpected and profound transformations. Everything happens for a reason. My worsening asthma and the sudden halt to my baseball dreams were devastating at the time, but they made room for something far greater—the joy and passion of playing the ukulele. I realize life happens for you, not to you. I had no control over what was happening to me, especially with my health and asthma. But I learned it had to happen to make room for something bigger. The ukulele became a source of hope, excitement, and fulfillment, transforming my outlook and giving me a new purpose.

## CALL TO ACTION

I challenge you to reflect on your adversities that were actually blessings in disguise. Consider the things or people you need to accept who have perhaps given you the wisdom, knowledge, and perspective you have today. Think about the challenges that pushed you out of your comfort zone and how they helped you grow. Recognize the priorities and values that have become clearer as a result of overcoming these challenges.

Take a moment to acknowledge the resilience you've built from facing difficulties and how they prepared you for future obstacles. Reflect on how these experiences have deepened your empathy and compassion toward others. Think about the unexpected opportunities that arose from your setbacks and how they enriched your life.

Embrace the journey and trust that each step, no matter how challenging, is leading you toward a greater purpose. By understanding and appreciating the hidden blessings, you can navigate life's unpredictability with a resilient spirit and an open heart.

The hidden blessings in my life gave me a new perspective, but also required me to break free from certain constraints. Breaking free from conventional expectations was essential for my growth, so let's now delve into how I learned to embrace my unique path.

www.DerickSebastian.com

# CHAPTER 4

# GETTING IN YOUR GAME

"Every strike brings me closer to the next home run."

— Babe Ruth

Have you ever had to decide between two passions and been unsure which path to take? How do you choose between a childhood dream and a newfound calling when both tug at your heart? What does it take to step up to the plate, overcome fear, and pursue what truly excites you? Can you find the courage to swing for the fences even when the outcome is uncertain?

## MY STORY

Growing up, baseball was my first love. My older brother Roger played and was considered one of the best in the state in high school. I admired his skill and dedication, and I found immense joy in the game. I loved the fundamentals and the mental approach that played such a big role. While playing, I have to admit I wasn't the most talented player on the field. Maybe you could say I was one of those average players who started and contributed but wasn't the star player.

I wasn't an aggressive, go-getter type either. I was timid. I wasn't the vocal leader who would rally my teammates and pump them up. In fact, to be honest, I used to get scared going up to bat. I was afraid of getting hit by the ball because I had seen my teammates get hit, and I had been beaned squarely in the ribs. It hurt so badly, like a huge cramp crawling through my midsection. That experience stayed with me and made me wary every time I stepped up to the plate.

Eventually, I learned baseball doesn't start with fundamentals; it starts in your mind. Your approach is all psychological. I had to learn how to be confident and believe if I thought I could be a great baseball player, I would become one. Building that confidence was challenging, but I chipped away at it every day before stepping onto the field for practice. For games, I would spend an hour before leaving the house visualizing success and going through all the necessary fundamentals.

My strength in baseball was defense. I played third base and outfield, but eventually, I became primarily a catcher. I loved playing defense because I always believed, though maybe I was a bit biased, "Defense wins games because without it, you can't stay in the game."

My weakness? Hitting. The fear of getting beaned was a significant part of my problem. I had to work on overcoming my fear of getting hit by the ball. I had to toughen up, primarily in my mind, so I thought, *I'm not going to get hit by the ball; I'm the one who's going to hit the ball!*

I eventually started developing confidence every time I went up to bat. I focused on the fundamentals of hitting, like keeping my weight on my back foot, not dropping my back shoulder, and swinging level to hit the top half of the ball and avoid pop flies. The process was long, so I had to learn patience. But when the ball came into my strike zone, I thought of myself as a slingshot, bringing the bat to the ball. Bam! I started getting solid, good hits.

Over time, I got consistent with these hitting fundamentals. I started getting on base more often by being a disciplined hitter, drawing walks, or hitting singles. With each success, my confidence grew, and I felt myself improving.

I became a very good contact hitter. Not the most powerful, but someone who could consistently put the ball in play. Eventually, I started getting bigger hits, like doubles and triples. And, yes, I began thinking about that elusive home run.

But no matter how hard I tried, it just didn't happen. I kept my head down, maintained a balanced stance, kept my weight on my back foot, and drove from the hips, swinging level and leading with my hands. I did everything right, but no home run. I had some great hits, but none went over the fence.

Then, one day, while playing in an off-island tournament in Hilo, our team was in a very close game. It was intense, and I found myself up to bat with one goal in mind: get on base. The pitcher wasn't giving me the pitch I wanted but throwing off-speed curves and changeups. I took a few pitches outside the strike zone, knowing he would eventually have to come into my zone. I took a deep breath and got into the batter's box. Then the pitcher threw a fastball down the pipe, waist-high, right in my strike zone.

Everything came together automatically: I kept my balance, loaded up on my back foot, opened my hips, led with my hands, and BAM! It was a solid hit deep into left center. I knew it was good.

My teammates were screaming and so was the crowd. I had one thing in mind: I needed to get to second base to get that double. I kept my head down and ran as fast as I could. As I rounded first base, the umpire told me to slow down. I was confused. Maybe it was a dead ball or foul ball? No way—I knew I had hit it hard in play. Then, the umpire smiled and gave me the signal, raising his right hand in the air and pointing to the sky in a circular motion. Wait, what? Really? That signal meant a home run! Are you sure? I hit a home run? I didn't slow down until I hit second base because I didn't believe it. But no defensive players were moving. All eyes were on me as I jogged around third base and eventually stepped on home plate to be greeted by my teammates and a cheering crowd.

The feeling of hitting a home run is something I will never forget. Although I never saw the ball go over the fence, the sense of accomplishment was incredible. "I did it." That was the only home run I ever hit in all my years of playing baseball. I never hit another one. I had plenty of singles, doubles, and triples, but no more home runs.

This experience was similar to my musical journey. I've made strides and hit many singles, doubles, and triples. The only difference is I feel I've hit more home runs in music than in baseball.

The truth is life isn't about home runs. It's about getting the opportunity to get up, off the bench, and get an at-bat. If you keep trying and making the best of your opportunities, everything will fall into place. First you'll get those small hits—the singles and doubles—and eventually, you'll work your way up to the exciting triples. Then, sooner or later, you'll hit your home run.

Like in baseball, you might walk or get a single, which is like landing smaller gigs and parties in music. But if you keep focusing on getting more at-bats and take advantage of those opportunities, you might hit a double or even a triple, like landing a big-paying gig or an inter-island show. Eventually, if you consistently keep getting at-bats, hitting singles, doubles, and triples, and simply getting on base, that home run will come. I've hit many in my music career, from going on music tours around the world to performing the national anthem on national sports stages, getting featured all over the news, and landing music licensing placements.

You, my friend, have to want to get in the game. You have to find a way to get off the bench and get your chance to bat. It's scary because you might feel you're not good enough or that coming off the bench is unfair because you're not getting as much playing time as the starters. But that's just an excuse. When you get in the game, make the best of it, and do your best. Whether you fail or succeed doesn't matter. At that point, the results don't matter. The opportunity does. You just want a chance to get in the game because if you keep trying, getting off the bench, and getting your at-bats, you will eventually get your singles, doubles, triples, and yes, your home run.

Getting in the game means stepping up to the plate despite your fears and doubts. It means seizing the opportunities that come your way and making the most of them. It means persevering through the challenges and setbacks, knowing that each at-bat is a chance to learn, grow, and improve.

When you're in the game, you're actively participating in your journey. You're not sitting on the sidelines, waiting for things to happen. You're taking action, making decisions, and pushing forward. You're building momentum with every swing, every hit, and every run.

So, whether you're pursuing a career in music, sports, or any other field, remember the key to success is getting in the game. Embrace the challenges, celebrate the small victories, and keep pushing forward. With persistence, determination, and a positive mindset, you can achieve your dreams and hit your home runs.

Step up to the plate, my friend. It's time to start getting in your game.

## WHAT I LEARNED

My music journey has been a lot like baseball. I needed to find a way just to get in the game because being on the bench wasn't doing me any good. I had to look for an "at-bat," an opportunity. Just like in baseball where every at-bat is a chance to prove yourself, in music I needed to find gigs that would let me perform my craft and help me get better. It didn't matter if the gigs were small or unpaid; what mattered was they got me off the bench and into the game.

Each performance, no matter how small, was like getting on base. It was a chance to show my skills, to connect with an audience, and to build my confidence. Every gig was an opportunity to improve and refine my craft, much like how each swing of the bat in baseball is a chance to perfect your technique. The more I performed, the more I learned, and the better I became.

Just like in baseball, where you start with small hits like singles and doubles, my music career began with small gigs. These were my practice sessions, my time to learn the ropes and understand the industry. I played at local events, small venues, and community gatherings. Each of these experiences was invaluable. They were my steppingstones, my way of getting in the game and staying in the game.

As I gained more experience and confidence, I started landing better gigs— my doubles and triples. These were bigger venues, more prestigious events, and higher-paying opportunities. With each success, my confidence grew, and so did my reputation. I was no longer just getting by; I was making a name for myself.

But just as in baseball, where the ultimate goal is to hit a home run, in music, the goal is to reach those pinnacle moments that define your career. For me, those home runs came in the form of international tours, performing the national anthem at major sports events, and having my music featured on national platforms. Each of these achievements was the result of years of hard work, persistence, and a willingness to take every opportunity, no matter how small, to get in the game.

The key lesson I learned is success doesn't come from sitting on the bench. Whether you're pursuing a career in music, sports, or any other field, remember the journey starts with getting in the game. Embrace every opportunity, no matter how small, and use it as a steppingstone to greater success. Keep swinging, keep striving, and one day, you'll hit those home runs you've been dreaming of. This is the essence of getting in your game.

**EXERCISE**

1. Getting in the Game

   - Question: Are you ready to get off the bench and into the batter's box of your life?

   - Activity: Create a mind map outlining your current situation and the specific steps needed to get in the game. Include your goals, potential obstacles, and any resources you can leverage.

   - Reflection: How does visualizing your journey help clarify your path? Reflect on the emotions and thoughts that arise as you map the steps you need to take to get in the game.

   _____

   _____

   _____

   _____

   _____

   _____

   _____

   _____

   _____

   _____

2.  Overcoming Fear through Visualization

    - Question: How can you transform your biggest fears into actionable confidence in your pursuits?

    - Activity: Practice a guided visualization exercise where you imagine overcoming your biggest fear and succeeding. Repeat this visualization daily for a week.

    - Reflection: After a week, reflect on any changes in your confidence and mindset. How has this practice influenced your approach to your goals?

    _____

    _____

    _____

    _____

    _____

    _____

    _____

3.  Building on Small Successes

    - Question: Can you identify a recent "single" or "double" you can build on to achieve greater success?

- Activity: Write a detailed account of a recent accomplishment and analyze the factors that contributed to it. Develop a plan to replicate or build upon these factors for future achievements.

- Reflection: How does acknowledging and analyzing your smaller successes motivate you to aim for bigger goals? Reflect on the next steps in building on this momentum.

_____

_____

_____

_____

_____

_____

_____

4.  Embracing Opportunities and Persistence

- Question: Which opportunities are you hesitating to take, and how can you step up to them more fearlessly? How have patience and resilience shaped your journey?

- Activity: List opportunities you've been hesitant to pursue, identifying fears or doubts holding you back, and develop a plan to address them. Write a narrative about an experience where patience and resilience were key to your success.

- Reflection: Reflect on how facing your fears and embracing opportunities could change your journey. Write about the lessons learned from past challenges and how you can apply them to your current goals.

_____

_____

_____

_____

_____

_____

_____

## FIVE TIPS FOR GETTING INTO YOUR GAME

1.  **Overcome Fear with Preparation:** Just as athletes visualize success and prepare mentally, you can conquer your fears by preparing and visualizing your goals. Mental preparation can transform anxiety into confidence, helping you face challenges head-on.

2.  **Consistent Practice and Mastery of Fundamentals:** Success in any field comes from consistent practice and a strong foundation in the basics. Whether you're improving your skills at work, in a hobby, or in personal development, focus on practicing regularly and mastering the fundamentals.

3.  **Embrace Incremental Progress:** Remember every small step counts toward your ultimate goal. Celebrate your incremental progress, knowing each minor achievement is a building block for greater success.

4. **Seize Opportunities Fearlessly:** Life presents numerous opportunities, and it's essential to embrace them despite any initial fears. Every chance you take is a potential game-changer, so step up and seize the moment with confidence.

5. **Cultivate Resilience and Patience:** Achieving significant goals requires resilience and patience. Understand setbacks are part of the journey and persist through the challenges. Your dedication will eventually lead to remarkable successes.

## SUMMARY

In this chapter, I drew parallels between my experiences in baseball and my musical career to highlight lessons in overcoming fear, embracing practice, and seizing opportunities. I learned success starts with the right mindset and visualizing success. This approach, coupled with relentless practice, led me to hit my first and only home run—an unforgettable milestone. I also emphasize life's similarity to baseball, pointing out it isn't about hitting home runs every time but about stepping up to the plate when opportunities arise. It's all about being prepared for what's to come. By consistently taking "at-bats," I've succeeded in music and achieved personal growth. This shows the key to success is making the most of every chance to bat. Get in the game, embrace every opportunity, and continually strive to improve.

Being in the game is crucial, but what truly defines our journey is how we master the challenges we face. In the next chapter, we'll look at how to face and conquer some of life's biggest hurdles.

## CALL TO ACTION

Now it's your turn to step up to the plate. I challenge you to reflect on the areas where you're hesitant to take action, whether it's due to fear, doubt, or uncertainty. Just like in baseball, success doesn't come from waiting on the bench; it comes from taking those at-bats, no matter how daunting they may seem. Visualize your goals, commit to consistent practice, and seize every opportunity that comes your way. Embrace the process, knowing each swing, whether it results in a hit or a miss, brings you closer to achieving your dreams. Get in the game, and start making your mark.

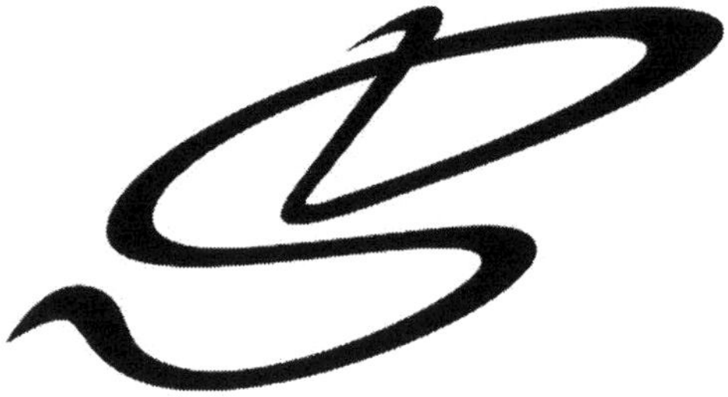

# SECTION 2:

# OVERCOMING YOUR CHALLENGES

"Strength doesn't come from what you can do.
It comes from overcoming the things you once thought you couldn't."

— Rikki Rogers

# DOWNLOAD AND STREAM SONG FOR FREE!

www.DerickSebastian.com/BecauseOfYou

# BECAUSE OF YOU

## Song Written and Performed by Derick Sebastian

This is us, here we are

We've got another day together

Being by your side is always better


I've got you, you've got me

Because of you I'm even stronger

I can stand a little taller


You taught me how to fly

To never give up and try

To be the best that I can be

Now I believe in me


It's because of you

It's because of you

I can make it through

In all I do

It's because of you

Now I can smile, and I can shine

Because of you my days are brighter

I can hold my head up higher


I won't fear, 'cause you're always near

This is another day together

And you by my side is always better

www.DerickSebastian.com

www.DerickSebastian.com

# CHAPTER 5

# BREAKING YOUR BROOMSTICK

"In every season of life, there is a purpose and a reason for growth."

— Lailah Gifty Akita

D o some situations, people, jobs, or rules make you feel trapped? Do they limit your creativity, crush your spirit, and diminish your passion?

**MY STORY**

My life got very interesting in eighth grade. I had been playing the ukulele for two years while also taking band class since the sixth grade, playing the trombone. While I still had a huge interest in the ukulele, band class gave me a new perspective on music. I learned to read music, understand time signatures, and play in sync with others. I believed I did pretty well with the trombone—in fact, after my first year in band, I was first seat trombone. I was actually shocked!

As I entered eighth grade band class, I suddenly felt a little confused, sort of at a crossroads. I excelled at learning the ukulele, playing by ear, and exploring techniques. I was free to improvise and played with emotion and expression. But I felt restricted in band class because it was all about reading music, sticking to time signatures, and being bound to the sheet music throughout the song. I didn't feel free. I was confused. Here I was involved in two music avenues: the experimental and freewheeling nature of the ukulele and the discipline and precision of the trombone—both offered completely different experiences. The ukulele was fun; the trombone wasn't.

I decided to take a different approach in band class to make it fun like playing the ukulele. I thought, *This is my last year in band class; how can I make it fun?* So, I took on a small secret mission.

I memorized all the sheet music, from top to bottom. I refused to rely on sheet music. I wanted to play my trombone like I played my ukulele, all by ear and from the heart. Throughout the week, I spent my time in band class figuring out all the songs' notes, timing, and feeling. I would memorize it, and when it was time for a band performance, the sheet music was merely a decoy. I enjoyed playing trombone by ear, ultimately, by feel and heart, just like the ukulele. Playing this way gave me the sense of being creative and free. The music felt more real, authentic, and a lot more moving.

Playing by heart made band class fun again. The concerts were super-awesome and free flowing, and learning new songs was a blast. But then, a little bird or two found out what I was doing and things went south. One day in band class, my teacher said, "Hey, Derick, can I see you after class?"

When the bell rang, I slowly walked up to the podium where he stood.

"Wait. Please get your trombone as well," he said. I quickly turned around to get my instrument and started walking back to him. I could see something was up by his laser beam stare that was just waiting to make eye contact with me.

He pulled out a new piece of music. "Here you go," he said. "I want you to play this right now, all by sight."

I was caught. I couldn't do it like a "first seat" should. He asked, "Are you just memorizing the music and not playing by sight?" I softly said, "Yes." Then he stressed how important it was to read my music note for note. I nodded in agreement just to get out of that super-awkward moment.

The next day, I was third seat trombone.

It sucked that I had been caught, but I didn't feel I had done anything wrong. I simply wanted to have fun in my own way playing the trombone. But I felt like someone had popped my band balloon—I was deflated, and band wasn't as fun anymore. Band class became more work than fun. I was bored just doing my best to read music and play note for note, so I eventually turned all my energy and focus back to the ukulele.

I had so much fun being curious with the ukulele. I practiced every day, but it didn't feel like work; it wasn't boring. Playing the ukulele was fulfilling. It gave me a natural high, exciting me so much I couldn't wait to pick up the instrument every day. You could certainly say I was obsessed with the ukulele.

I decided to really commit to the ukulele and see where it would take me. How this super-cool, four-string, little instrument was changing my life soon became much clearer.

Mr. Ellis and I got really close. He was like my best friend, my *hanai* (adopted) dad. I really looked forward to going to school because I got to hang out with Mr. Ellis and play ukulele.

Mr. Ellis pulled me out in the middle of classes more than a few times. He'd say he needed to talk to me, but we ended up going to the locker rooms to jam ukulele. Although it surely wasn't the logical or right thing to do, emotionally, it was the right thing to do. As long as my grades were top-notch, straight As, Mr. Ellis let me do this. Actually, it happened fairly often. Heck, he was the school security guard, so it seemed like I was some sort of troublemaker, but as long as I was doing well in school, he was okay with me cutting class.

Mr. Ellis and I took a step forward and decided to play for my eighth-grade class during lunch. We were on the stage, mic'd up, and actually doing a real performance. That was my first performance. I was so nervous and hesitant, but it was one of the best feelings ever. It was so fun. After, we decided to enter a few local talent competitions on Maui.

The ukulele was becoming part of me. I wanted to do more, and the Universe answered in a very weird way. I was riding in the car with my mom, casually listening to KCCN FM100, a popular local radio station based on Oahu, when I heard a catchy advertisement about a statewide ukulele contest on Oahu. I was so excited I called the radio station to find out more. They said I needed to be at least thirteen and submit a recording of an original ukulele instrumental song. If selected, I would be flown to

Oahu to perform it live for the semifinal round. If I made it to the top three, I would be flown back to Oahu for the finals.

I was so excited! I went to Mr. Ellis to pitch him the idea of entering this statewide ukulele competition. Mr. Ellis was just as excited as I was. It was on!

We sat down, brainstormed long and hard, and wrote and arranged a song called "Magic Room," named after an office in our school's PE locker room where we had our ukulele jam sessions. It was a long and interesting collaboration because I was the solo ukulele performer, and Mr. Ellis served as a cowriter and facilitator. Mr. Ellis was not gifted as a complex ukulele player, but he was gifted with an ear. So, to collaborate, he would hear an idea and sound it out with his mouth. Then I would figure out how to play it on the ukulele, all by ear. Understand, we had no real musical training—everything was done by ear, patterns, and techniques.

We practiced for hours throughout the week, trying to arrange the composition the best we could. I got tired and a little burnt out, but I kept pushing and showing up because I knew we had a mission to accomplish.

I was all in, laser-focused on this ukulele mission, and it became obvious to my classmates. They saw me practicing all the time, performing on stage. Eventually, they learned Mr. Ellis and I were composing a song for a statewide ukulele contest. With the extra attention, I got a taste of "teen drama" that really disrupted my focus. Some of my classmates started to talk crap about me—more than I expected. They said I was conceited and thought I was better than others. I can say this from my heart: I had no intention of making others feel like that. The truth is, I kept to myself and never bothered anyone. I went to class, did my best, respected my classmates, and played ukulele. That was it. Nothing more, nothing less.

"Haters are a good problem to have. Nobody hates
the good ones; they hate the great ones!"

— Kobe Bryant

This unwanted drama started playing with my mind, and I started to worry what others thought about me. I honestly felt that playing ukulele was wrong. Maybe I had to do what my other classmates were doing: just hang around and talk crap? Not really do anything creative except school and sports? Maybe I should conform to what a "normal" thirteen-year-old would be doing? I was hurt, confused, and starting to feel uneasy about the entire mission.

Then one afternoon, I was sitting at the table in the PE locker room across from Mr. Ellis, our usual spot. We were going over "Magic Room," reviewing all the difficult picking parts we had written over the previous days. I was unfocused, unmotivated, and making tons of mistakes. Mr. Ellis got so upset he suddenly grabbed a broom that happened to be next to him and WHAP!

He hit the desk with the broomstick so hard it snapped in half.

I was shocked—not scared, startled. But after a few seconds, I was pretty impressed and thought, How cool is it for someone to break a broomstick on a desk! I had never seen it before. But no, I didn't say a word.

Mr. Ellis made me put away my ukulele. Then he asked, "Why are you so unfocused and making so many mistakes?"

I couldn't help telling the truth. I wasn't swift enough to make up a story, so everything came out. I told him how my classmates were talking crap and spreading all kinds of rumors about me. We had a long, deep conversation. He made it clear this adversity would only help me grow and become a better person.

The conversation is still so clear in my mind. "First of all," Mr. Ellis said, "you're wasting my time. The one thing you need to have in life is consideration of others' time. You need to make time count, especially if you have a commitment and goal to accomplish. Second, if what others are saying about you isn't true, don't believe or even listen to it because it's just noise. You can't control what others do, but you can control what you do. We have the opportunity of a lifetime to write a song that can change our lives. We're being productive. And your classmates who are busy talking crap and spreading rumors are not. Let them talk because, at the end of the day, our results will speak for themselves."

It was the talk I desperately needed to reset.

I regained my focus, and we finished writing "Magic Room" some weeks later. I recorded it on a cassette tape via my brother's boombox—yes, you read that correctly, we went "old school."

I submitted the song.

We were surprised a few months later when we received a letter stating our song was selected as one of the top six, so we were invited to perform the song live at the preliminaries on Oahu at Ward Warehouse.

After, we couldn't believe it when we were selected to be among the top three finalists for the ukulele division contest. We were advancing to the Hawaii state finals.

Mr. Ellis and I flew back to Oahu for our second round—it was finally time for the finals. We prayed deeply together before my performance. I was so nervous. The night went on, but all I really heard were two roars from the audience. The first was after my performance of "Magic Room," and the second giant roar was when they announced, "Ladies and gentlemen, the winner of this year's solo ukulele division competition is: Derick Sebastian!"

The process had been long, nearly a year and a half from creating and submitting the song to winning, but there we were. Mr. Ellis had been my right-hand man on this song—we did it. We made it; we won the entire statewide ukulele competition! At fifteen years old, I was a state champion!

In everyone's eyes it was a solo performance, but it was a team effort, mentored and led by Mr. Ellis.

We were awarded our first recording contract. We flew back to Oahu to specifically record "Magic Room" and a bonus song, one of the all-time great theme songs, "Pink Panther," in which I collaborated with Jake Shimabukuro. (This was before he became famous with his Pure Heart Band.) What an experience.

Looking back, I realize my journey was not just about playing the ukulele but about embracing the challenges and breaking free from restrictions. It was about finding my own path and expressing myself authentically. When Mr. Ellis broke that broomstick, it freed me from self-doubt and others' judgment to follow my own vision for my future.

## WHAT I LEARNED

When you're curious and venture down your own path, trying new things, people will always have opinions and may even try to bring you down. That can be difficult to cope with, but it's important to look at the bigger picture. Be willing to grow, find your way, develop close relationships, and trust that whatever you're doing is just part of your becoming.

Time is of the essence; it's something we can never get back. Making the most of your time, especially when pursuing your passions, is crucial. Use every moment to learn, grow, and move closer to your dreams. Embrace the challenges and the noise from others as part of your journey, knowing they are helping to shape you into who you are meant to be.

## EXERCISE

1.  Reflecting on Pivotal Moments

    - Question: Have you experienced a "breaking your broomstick" moment where distractions or criticism challenged your progress? How did you push through and succeed in your own unique way?

    - Activity: In your journal, reflect on moments when you faced distractions or criticism and how you overcame them.

    - Reflection: How do these reflections help you understand your resilience and determination?

    _____

    _____

_____

_____

2.  Reframing Setbacks as Growth Opportunities

    • Question: How can you reframe a recent setback or challenge as an
      opportunity for personal growth? What strategies can you employ
      to maintain focus and determination?

    • Activity: Visualize a recent setback and imagine yourself
      overcoming it. Role-play scenarios where you face criticism or
      distraction.

    • Reflection: How does visualizing success and practicing responses
      change your mindset and prepare you for real-life situations?

    _____

    _____

    _____

    _____

3.  Leveraging Support and Mentorship

    • Question: How can you channel setbacks or failures into motivation
      for future success? Who are your mentors or supporters, and how
      can you leverage their guidance during tough times?

- Activity: Write a letter to a mentor expressing gratitude for their guidance.

- Reflection: How does acknowledging your mentors' influence reinforce their lessons and help you navigate challenges?

_____

_____

_____

_____


4. Balancing Structure and Creativity

- Question: How do you balance structured learning with creative expression? What recent accomplishment or progress are you proud of? How can you celebrate it?

- Activity: Identify an area where you feel restricted and brainstorm ways to incorporate more creativity and freedom. Create a plan to celebrate your recent accomplishments or progress.

- Reflection: How does balancing structure and creativity enhance fulfillment and motivation? How does celebrating your achievements boost your self-worth?

_____

_____

_____

_____

## FIVE TIPS FOR EMBRACING YOUR "BREAKING YOUR BROOMSTICK" MOMENT

1. **Embrace Adversity as Growth:** When you face moments of adversity, see them as opportunities for growth and self-discovery. Just as breaking the broomstick symbolized frustration, use your challenges as catalysts to push yourself farther and grow stronger.

2. **Stay Focused on Your Goals:** Despite distractions and criticism from others, stay focused on your goals. Make every moment count toward achieving your commitments and dreams, regardless of the noise around you. Your dedication will help you stay on track.

3. **Turn Setbacks into Comebacks:** When setbacks happen, use them as fuel for comebacks. Instead of letting negativity drag you down, let it motivate you to prove your abilities. Channel your frustrations into determination and resilience.

4. **Value Mentorship and Support:** Appreciate the guidance and support of mentors and those who believe in you. Surround yourself with people who encourage you to reach your potential, especially during challenging times. Their wisdom and encouragement can help you navigate difficulties and stay focused on your path.

5. **Celebrate Achievements:** Celebrate your achievements and milestones along the way. Acknowledge your successes and the progress you've made despite the obstacles. Each victory, no matter how small, is a testament to your resilience and determination.

## SUMMARY

On your journey of self-discovery and pursuit of your passions, it's natural to encounter obstacles and face criticism. When you do, remain true to yourself and your aspirations. Remain focused on your goals and beliefs. Mr. Sam Ellis III played a pivotal role for me not only as an ukulele instructor but as a mentor, confidant, and father figure. He helped me believe in myself and strive for excellence. Together, we learned to turn setbacks into comebacks, value the journey of self-discovery, and celebrate achievements. Through his mentorship, I discovered the true essence of success—staying true to yourself, overcoming obstacles, and embracing the journey with gratitude and tenacity.

Breaking free from traditional constraints allowed me to pursue my passions more fully. However, this journey wasn't without its challenges. In the next chapter, we'll explore the pursuit of seemingly unattainable dreams and the relentless drive needed to chase them.

## CALL TO ACTION

I challenge you to reflect on your "breaking your broomstick" moment and embrace it, not reject it. How have you grown from the experience? Were there setbacks—or even deeper, and are they still holding you back today? Embrace these moments as opportunities to grow and continue to move forward with resilience and determination.

www.DerickSebastian.com

# CHAPTER 6

# PURSUING YOUR UNATTAINABLE GOALS

"You have to dream before your dreams can come true."

— A. P. J. Abdul Kalam

Have you ever stood at a crossroads, faced with a decision that could change the course of your life? How do you choose between a childhood dream and a newfound passion when both pull at your heart? What would you do if following your passion meant leaving behind something familiar and safe? Could you trust your gut feeling when the path ahead seems uncertain, yet undeniably exciting?

## MY STORY

High school seems like a blur. I became healthy enough to return to playing sports and got into baseball, football, and even ran track. I had a great run in sports, especially baseball, and I imagined taking it to the next level. Maybe playing in college? But the nudge wasn't as strong as my musical calling.

Entering my senior year, I had to decide—take my chances and maybe further my career in baseball by playing college ball, or go all in and pursue the music thing? But wait; if I didn't try to play college baseball, how would I fulfill my childhood dream of becoming a MLB player? It was a difficult crossroad.

I had to choose. Something told me I should go for music. I don't know what it was, but music was more exciting to me. I went all in, dropping out of sports my senior year to concentrate on music. Yes, a lot of my friends, teammates, and coaches were disappointed, but I listened to my gut.

I joined a trio called "Island Sounds," and boy, we made the best of it. We put on seventy shows in just nine months—that was a lot, especially since two of the three of us were still in high school. But it was a complete blast. We played at parties, weddings, private events, festivals, concerts, late-night clubs, and even traveled throughout the neighboring islands to do shows.

It was such a crazy and fun time. Our band was always on the move. By the time I realized it was time for a reality check, I was graduating as part of the class of 2000.

Being at graduation, surrounded by classmates for the last time, was pretty emotional. I honestly don't like graduations. They are the big step into reality, into a new chapter in our lives. Whether you're ready or not, you have to grow up and make a move. Either go to college or start working, or even do both. Simple, yet not simple. Most eighteen-year-olds don't seem ready for this step. We just don't know what we want to do or what we want to be. For me, the decision was whether I should go to college and study for something I wasn't sure I really wanted to do, or keep on keeping on with my music.

I chose music once again. I went to Los Angeles with a big dream of becoming an ukulele star. I moved to Hollywood to attend The Los Angeles Recording School. I learned all aspects of music production. It was so much fun. I met a lot of great people, and I grew up quickly by learning to live in such an overwhelming city. I tried to book gigs, but at the time, I wasn't really a solo performer since I was coming out of a trio. I tried to make deeper connections in the music scene, but it all led to late-night clubs and bars, which really didn't fit my vibe. I also had aspirations of working as an audio engineer in the huge entertainment and sports world in LA, but that didn't pan out either. I even tried getting into UCLA's music extension program but no luck. After finishing up at The Los Angeles Recording School, I had nowhere else to go but back home to Maui. Even though it was a great two-year run in LA, I fell short of my dream of becoming an ukulele star.

Back in Maui, I immediately started playing restaurant gigs and found a weekend residence at one of the coolest west side beaches on Maui, Hula Grill Kaanapali. It was great, but society told me to do more. So, I went through the motions of being a college student at Maui College. I eventually graduated with an Associate of Arts degree and headed into my four-year degree in Human Relations.

I kept the music gigs during these years, but I tried my best to put this "college" expectation first. I just didn't feel like I was on the path to fulfillment. A year away from graduating, I was just over it. I couldn't see myself going to school any longer. I decided to find a job and pursue my music once more. I was working as an educational assistant and trying to find more gigs outside of the Hula Grill, but that was it. Nothing more, nothing less. My music wasn't getting me where I had hoped.

I was frustrated, really frustrated, wondering why my music wasn't working. I was confused because I had worked so hard on my music, but I wasn't getting my break or more opportunities. I started to compare myself to other, younger local artists, people I helped get started in their careers. Now they were getting the bigger concert gigs, releasing CDs, and getting their songs played over the radio. They were "making it," and I wasn't. What was I doing wrong? All the signs told me just to call it quits with my music. I was in a rut, thinking maybe I was simply not good enough, regardless of how far I'd come with the ukulele—music seemed like it just simply wasn't the plan.

But during this unfulfilling time with my music career, I found a silver lining. My longtime high school sweetheart Raymi and I started talking about marriage. As that conversation lingered on for several months, we found ourselves pregnant with our first baby.

Raymi and I were married on December 19, 2004. Shortly after, we were a young married couple with a newborn son named Santana, born on June 9, 2005. When we bought a home, I realized this was real. I was now responsible for raising my own family. I wanted to be a good husband and father—I expected a lot of myself.

Although this new journey as a family man included some exciting times, as reality set in, I felt like my dream of becoming a successful ukulele artist was over. How could I chase a music dream when I was responsible for a family? I needed to work daily at a job, take care of the baby, be a faithful husband, take care of the house, cars, etc. My music dream was doomed.

Don't get me wrong; it was one of the most beautiful times in my life, but I still felt something was missing.

After about a year of going through multiple jobs and putting my music on the far backseat, life became really frustrating. I wasn't happy with what I was doing. I truly felt I was wasting my time and efforts. I knew deep down inside there had to be more. One morning while carrying my son, I had my "come to Jesus" moment. The thought came in loud and clear: How am I supposed to encourage my child to live out his life's calling and go after his dream when his own father isn't doing it? Just because I was a young husband and father didn't mean I needed to conform to the world's usual path and expectations of going to school, getting a degree, starting a family, finding a job, being an employee until I was sixty-five, and then retiring. The path society had instilled in me did not reflect the true to me.

I prayed hard about it, and with the blessings of my wife, Raymi, I took a leap of faith. In August 2006, I quit all my jobs and became a full-time musician, primarily doing gigs at the Hula Grill, lobby lounges, small private parties, and luau shows. It was a slow start, and the money wasn't the best, but I knew I had to go after my dreams if I wanted to teach Santana how to go after his.

I ended up investing in myself and my music business, working with industry professionals, music coaches, and mentors, learning marketing and branding, and how to present myself as a major label music artist. I started branching out, going to music conferences and training in Los Angeles (Music Strategies by Tim Sweeney).

I became a motivated working machine. My daily routine was waking up at 3:30 a.m. before Santana woke at six, working on the music business, website, social media (do you remember Myspace?), emails, artists' profiles, and promotional materials, music demos, and pitching for more gigs and music festivals throughout the US. I developed a non-negotiable mindset that if I can dream it, I can achieve it.

I felt like a new me, and I was on a personal mission. I eventually gained momentum and started getting more music opportunities. My demo songs were being played on the local radio, and I was doing radio interviews. I was expanding more as a performing ukulele artist at hotels, corporate events, weddings, and ukulele festivals throughout the US. It was slowly happening. I was living my dream, with a greater purpose, while raising my beautiful family.

Was it the way I envisioned it? Not at all, but every twist and turn led me to exactly where I needed to be. Each unexpected detour shaped my path and reinforced my belief in the power of pursuing one's passion. This was my journey of pursuing unattainable goals.


**WHAT I LEARNED**

Everything happens for a reason. My plan is great, but God's plan is greater, and if it was meant to be, it will be in God's perfect time. I've come to understand that while we can set our sights on our dreams and work tirelessly toward them, sometimes the Universe has its own timeline. It's essential to trust the process and have faith things will unfold as they are meant to.

On my journey, I've faced moments of doubt and frustration, where it seemed my dreams were slipping away. But each setback set me up for something greater. The detours, the pauses, and even the disappointments were all part of a bigger picture I couldn't see at the moment. They were necessary steps, guiding me toward a destiny more fulfilling than I ever could have imagined.

I've learned to embrace patience and see the beauty in waiting. In those quiet moments of uncertainty I've found my strength, resilience, and a deeper connection to my purpose. Every challenge has taught me valuable lessons, preparing me for the opportunities that eventually came my way. Trusting in a higher plan allowed me to let go of control, surrender to the flow of life, and appreciate the journey, not just the destination.

When you find yourself questioning your path or feeling impatient about your progress, remember there's a bigger plan at work. Have faith that everything is aligning perfectly, even if it doesn't seem like it right now. Keep pushing forward, stay true to your dreams, and trust that the timing will always be right in the end. That is the essence of pursuing your unattainable goals.

**EXERCISE**

1.  Visualizing and Prioritizing Your Dreams

    - Question: What is your "impossible dream," and how can you prioritize your passion over societal expectations to take a leap toward it?

- Activity: Create a vision board representing your dream using images, words, and symbols that inspire you. Then, write a letter to yourself outlining the steps you will take to prioritize your passion and align your actions with your dreams.

- Reflection: How does visualizing your dream and committing your plans to writing enhance your motivation and belief in your dream's attainability, and encourage you to act?

_____

_____

_____


2. Navigating Life's Crossroads

- Question: How do you navigate life's crossroads and make decisions that align with your dreams?

- Activity: Develop a decision-making framework that includes your core values, long-term goals, and potential outcomes. Use it to evaluate a current or past crossroads.

- Reflection: How does this framework help you make decisions that are true to your dreams and values?

_____

_____

_____

3.  Overcoming Self-Doubt and Cultivating Confidence

    •  Question: How do you overcome self-doubt and keep moving forward in the pursuit of your dreams?

    •  Activity: Create a list of affirmations and positive statements to recite daily. Write down your core purpose and why your dream is important to you.

    •  Reflection: How do these affirmations and reconnecting with your core purpose affect your mindset, resilience, and resolve when facing challenges?

    _____

    _____

    _____

    _____

4.  Cultivating Patience and Trust in the Process

    •  Question: How do you maintain faith and patience while waiting for your dreams to unfold in their own time?

    •  Activity: Practice mindfulness meditation, focusing on patience and trusting the process. Reflect on the feelings and insights that arise during meditation.

    •  Reflection: How does practicing mindfulness help you cultivate patience and maintain faith in your journey?

_____

_____

_____

_____

## FIVE TIPS FOR PURSUING YOUR UNATTAINABLE GOALS

1. **Follow Your Passion:** When facing uncertainty, choose to pursue what you are passionate about, even if it means stepping away from a conventional path. Your true calling will guide you to fulfillment.

2. **Embrace Life's Crossroads:** When confronted with choices between stability and the unknown, embrace the opportunity to explore new possibilities. Pursue your dreams courageously, even when the path is uncertain.

3. **Overcome Setbacks:** Understand that setbacks and feelings of inadequacy are part of the journey. Persevere and continue to chase your dreams, refusing to give up even when faced with challenges.

4. **Find Purpose:** Evaluate your priorities and let them guide your actions. Whether it's a new role in life or a personal commitment, use it as fuel to reignite your determination and set an example for those you care about.

5. **Trust in Divine Timing:** Practice prayer, reflection, or meditation to align with a higher purpose. Trust that everything happens for a reason and surrender to the timing of the Universe, knowing your path will unfold as it should.

## SUMMARY

In the pursuit of my dream, I faced numerous challenges and setbacks that led me to question the validity of my aspirations. Despite initial disappointments and detours, I discovered life's timing isn't always aligned with our plans. What we often perceive as setbacks are actually opportunities for growth and redirection. Embracing who I was, based on what life gave me, ultimately shaped me into the person I needed to be to pursue my dream wholeheartedly. Each experience, no matter how difficult, contributed to my personal and professional growth. The moments of doubt and frustration were steppingstones guiding me to a deeper understanding of my purpose and resilience.

Pursuing unattainable dreams requires more than vision—it also takes the courage to get in the game. It's about stepping onto the field and facing each challenge head-on. Next, let's look at how mastering my biggest challenges was a pivotal part of my journey.

## CALL TO ACTION

I challenge you to reflect on your own dreams and aspirations. Have setbacks or unexpected turns caused you to abandon your dreams prematurely? If your dream still ignites passion within, consider revisiting it and taking the necessary steps to make it a reality. Reconnect with what truly matters to you and embrace the journey with an open heart and mind. Remember, sometimes life's detours lead us to our true purpose. This is the journey of pursuing your unattainable goals.

www.DerickSebastian.com

# CHAPTER 7

# MASTERING YOUR BIGGEST CHALLENGES

"The world is a playground, now go out and play."

— Johnson Enos

What happens when winning isn't enough and the victories you once cherished lose their meaning? Can you shift your focus from short-term wins to long-term fulfillment? How do you define true success in the game of life, and are you ready to embrace the challenges that come with it?

## MY STORY

Growing up as the youngest of four, I felt like I had a lot to prove. Yes, I was the youngest and sort of knew I could get everything I wanted because I was spoiled in every way. I was Mama's boy. But still, I always had that little edge because I was always labeled the "baby." So, winning was everything. I wanted to win at hide-and-seek, milk caps, dodgeball, baseball, football, card games, classroom games—everything. I just hated losing; winning was everything.

Looking back, I realize winning all those games, challenges, and competitions, although it felt important at the time, wasn't everything. Winning those games was short-term. It provided just fleeting happiness.

Now that I am a little older and wiser, I know the most important game to win is the game of life. This game is not short-term; it's long-term. Playing it well goes beyond happiness to bring about a state of joy. Joy is being content, no matter what circumstances you are in, good or bad. Being in joy is accepting and acknowledging who you are right here, right now, and understanding where you want to be. Winning in the game of life includes unconditional love, honesty, faithfulness, thinking of others, forgiving, and doing what's right. In Hawaiian, we call this being *pono*.

There's a difference between "being right" and "doing right." Life is not always about "being" right; it is truly about "doing" right. Sometimes doing right is difficult; it's often outside your comfort zone. It's having a hard conversation. It's being honest and telling a hard truth. Short-term, it may not feel good because it's difficult, but long-term, it's beyond rewarding because it develops a foundation of character for all who are involved.

For example, I'm a father of three boys, and sometimes, it's difficult to constructively criticize them in everything they do—school, sports, character, life, etc. For the most part, when I'm honest and tell them the truth, they don't like it. They throw a fit, get mad, try to walk away, or even give me the silent treatment. But with a little compassion and patience, over time, and by explaining I was being honest because I simply love them and I'm looking out for the best in them, they accept the criticism and it helps them develop character. Most importantly, I remind them we are all growing together, learning together, and walking the journey of life together. This acknowledgment builds relationships, trust, and unconditional love.

Winning life is everything. To do that, you need to win every given day.

My uncle Earl always told me, "Head down, ass up. Work hard and don't ever let anyone stop you—no one! Always work hard in silence, and let your success be the noise."

The late great coach Fred Crowell always told me, "In order to win the day, you need to win every second, then win the minute, win the hour, and then win the day."

Winning the day doesn't mean every day will go your way or you'll always feel on top, although that definitely feels great. But winning does means going through adversity and challenges with a great attitude, accepting them, acknowledging them, and being present in them.

Simply put, it's about finding joy in every adversity. Why? Because you grow. You learn to accept, be in the moment, and let yourself feel the current state you are in, knowing it's not permanent, just temporary. Mistakes are not failures; they are lessons.

People will talk crap and gossip—accept it but let it go. People are entitled to their own opinions; whatever they say is whatever they say. You either believe it or not. But it's completely up to you how you handle the swirling nonsense that goes on every day.

Winning your day is about protecting yourself and being true to what you believe your calling is. It's about fighting to do what is right every single day. Winning is doing everything you can every day to somehow make progress in your given purpose. Winning means doing the uncomfortable, stepping outside of your comfort zone, making cold calls and sending emails, traveling to the unknowns, and taking that step forward even though you're scared out of your bones.

Winning is falling down nine times but getting up ten. Winning the game of life is everything. It's about showing up every day with the intention to be better than you were yesterday. It's about embracing the challenges and using them as steppingstones to greatness. It's about living with purpose, integrity, and relentless determination.

Many times in my musical career, I faced rejection after rejection. Venues would turn me down, managers would overlook me, and critics would doubt my abilities. Each rejection was a blow, but I learned to see them as lessons. I realized every "no" was pushing me closer to a "yes," and every failure was teaching me something valuable about perseverance, resilience, and self-belief. This mindset helped me transform setbacks into opportunities for growth and improvement.

Moreover, winning in life means building strong, meaningful relationships. It's about giving back to others, supporting your community, and being a positive influence. Success is not just measured by personal achievements but also by the influence you have on those around you. When you help others succeed, you create a ripple effect of positivity and success that benefits everyone.

Winning the game of life also involves continuous learning and self-improvement. It's about being curious, seeking knowledge, and being open to new experiences. This mindset keeps you adaptable and prepared for life's ever-changing landscape. Whether it's learning a new skill, embracing a new hobby, or taking on a new challenge, each experience adds to your growth and enriches your journey.

So, focus on winning your game of life by setting daily goals, maintaining a positive attitude, and being resilient in the face of adversity. That is how you truly win. And remember, every small victory leads to the ultimate triumph in mastering your biggest challenges.

## WHAT I LEARNED

Winning is not about being happy; it's about being joyful!

Happiness is fleeting; it's often dependent on external circumstances and temporary achievements. Happiness is that rush of excitement when you score a point, win a game, or receive praise. While those moments are wonderful, they are short-lived and can quickly fade when faced with the next challenge or setback.

Joy is a deeper, more enduring state. It's an inner sense of peace and contentment that persists regardless of external conditions. Joy comes from knowing who you are, embracing your journey, and finding meaning and purpose in your experiences. It's about being fully present in each moment, appreciating the process, and recognizing the growth that comes from both victories and defeats.

I've learned true joy comes from within. It can't be given or taken away by others. It's cultivated through self-awareness, gratitude, and a commitment to living authentically. Joy is waking up each day with a sense of purpose, knowing every step you take is part of a bigger, meaningful journey.

Joy is also about resilience. It's finding the silver lining in difficult situations and using challenges as opportunities to learn and grow. When you are joyful, you understand setbacks are not permanent obstacles but temporary detours leading to a stronger, wiser version of yourself. This mindset allows you to navigate life's ups and downs with grace and optimism.

Moreover, joy is about connection. It's found in the relationships we build, the love we share, and the positive influence we have on others. When we lift others up, we elevate ourselves. By supporting and encouraging those around us, we create a community of joy that nurtures and sustains us.

Winning the game of life, therefore, is not about accumulating accolades or achieving momentary happiness. It's about cultivating a deep sense of joy that endures through all of life's experiences. It's about being true to yourself, living with integrity, and finding fulfillment in the journey rather than the destination.

As I reflect on my own path, I see that the moments of true joy were not always times of public recognition or external success. They were often the quiet, personal victories—the times I overcame self-doubt, persevered through challenges, and stayed true to my values. Those moments have shaped who I am and brought me lasting joy.

In your own life, seek out joy rather than fleeting happiness. Embrace the journey with all its twists and turns, knowing each experience is a valuable part of your growth. Find joy in your passions, your relationships, and your personal achievements. And remember, winning the game of life is about being joyful, living with purpose, and cherishing each step along the way.

**EXERCISE**

1.  Overcoming Life's Biggest Challenges

    *   Question: Where do you struggle in beating life's biggest challenges, and how can you reframe them as opportunities for growth?

    *   Activity: Write a detailed account of your current challenges, identifying specific struggles and barriers. Then, reframe these challenges as opportunities to learn and build resilience.

    *   Reflection: Reflect on how this perspective shift influences your approach to challenges and your overall growth.

    _____

    _____

    _____

    _____

2.  Incorporating Continuous Improvement

    *   Question: How can you integrate continuous improvement into your daily routine for both personal and professional growth?

- Activity: Create a daily improvement plan with measurable goals for personal and professional development. Track your progress regularly.

- Reflection: Reflect on the changes you notice over time. How has focusing on continuous improvement affected your well-being and progress?

_____

_____

_____

3.  Acting with Integrity in Difficult Situations

- Question: Can you think of a situation where doing the right thing wasn't the easiest path? How did you or could you approach it with integrity?

- Activity: Identify a recent situation where you had to choose between the easy path and the right path. Write down the steps you took or could take to act with integrity.

- Reflection: Reflect on the outcomes of acting with integrity. How does this approach affect your relationships and self-worth?

_____

_____

_____

4.  Finding Joy and Purpose in Adversity

    •   Question: How can you find or create joy in a current or recent adversity and align more closely with your purpose?

    •   Activity: Practice gratitude by writing down three things you're grateful for each day, focusing on finding joy in adversity. Additionally, write a personal mission statement that aligns with your core values.

    •   Reflection: Reflect on how these practices influence your outlook and help you navigate tough times with positivity and purpose.

    _____

    _____

    _____

    _____

## FIVE TIPS FOR MASTERING YOUR BIGGEST CHALLENGES

1.  **Embrace Continuous Improvement:** Winning the game of life is about constant growth and improvement, not just in achievements but in character and spirit. Strive to be better each day, learning from every experience.

2.  **Prioritize Integrity and Doing Right:** Focus on doing what is right, especially when it's challenging. Prioritize integrity in your actions over simply being right. This builds strong character and lasting relationships.

3.  **Develop Resilience Through Challenges:** Approach each day with the mindset of overcoming adversity with a positive attitude. Your ability to bounce back from setbacks is key to mastering your biggest challenges.

4.  **Cultivate Joy in Adversity:** Find joy even in difficult times. This approach transforms temporary setbacks into valuable lessons and growth opportunities, helping you win the game of life and maintain a positive spirit.

5.  **Stay True to Your Purpose:** Protect your beliefs and pursue your purpose relentlessly. Let your core values guide you through challenges, ensuring you remain focused on what truly matters.

**SUMMARY**

In this chapter, I explored the profound realization that winning isn't solely about achieving momentary victories in games or competitions; it's about overcoming life's broader challenges and finding lasting joy. As I matured, I recognized life is the true game to win. This game isn't short-term; it's about developing resilience, acting with integrity, and maintaining joy through all of life's ups and downs. It's important to do what's right, not just be right, and know that honest, challenging conversations can strengthen relationships and build character. Daily victories are not about flawless days but about overcoming difficulties with a positive spirit and learning from each experience. True winning involves continuous growth, accepting and learning from criticism, and relentlessly pursuing one's purpose despite fear and discomfort.

Mastering challenges equips us for the varying seasons of life. Each season brings its own lessons and opportunities for growth. Next, let's explore how navigating these seasons has influenced my path.

## CALL TO ACTION

I challenge you to reflect on what winning means to you. Is it about short-term achievements or something deeper? Identify one area where you can apply the principle of doing right over being right, and take some small action toward this. How can you turn everyday challenges into opportunities to master your biggest challenges? Your answer will be the heart of mastering your biggest challenges.

www.DerickSebastian.com

# CHAPTER 8

# NAVIGATING YOUR LIFE'S GRIEF

"The most beautiful people we have known are those who have known defeat, known suffering, known struggle, known loss, and have found their way out of the depths. These persons have an appreciation, a sensitivity, and an understanding of life that fills them with compassion, gentleness, and a deep loving concern. Beautiful people do not just happen."

— Dr. Elisabeth Kübler-Ross

Have you ever experienced a moment of triumph that was suddenly overshadowed by unexpected loss? How do you find the strength to keep going when life throws you into a season of profound pain? Can you embrace the challenges that come with each season of life and continue to move forward? What does it take to navigate through these difficult times while holding on to the lessons and love that shape who you are?

## MY STORY

In 2013, I was "breaking through" the ukulele world. It was an exciting period, and I could feel the momentum. I started to tour internationally. I was on a three-country tour. After I finished a tour in Australia, I began a three-country tour of Thailand, the Philippines, and South Korea. Thailand was an eye-opener, with its rich Asian culture and endless activities. I had never seen so many people at once, and the traffic almost gave me a heart attack. But nonetheless, it was fun and a great experience! And the Philippines? Wow! It was special because that's where my mom and dad are from. I felt a deep connection, and it was a humbling experience to share my gift of music in the place where my family began. I was on television commercials and billboards—it was insane! The treatment was first class, and I was blown away that all of this was happening simply from playing my ukulele!

But then I received a heart-wrenching phone call. Mr. Ellis's health had taken a terrible turn. He was in the hospital and not doing well. He was declining rapidly, and I was thousands of miles away from the man who had changed my life. Fortunately, the tour allowed me to return home to Maui for five days before the next leg. I was relieved to see him, although not so relieved to see him bedridden with barely any response.

The third day I was home, I was doing house chores and planning to visit the hospital later when I got a phone call. Mr. Ellis had tried to sit up in bed and immediately gone into cardiac arrest. I rushed out of the house, got in the car, and sped to the hospital. No matter how fast my blood and mind were racing, everything felt like slow motion. By the time I got to his room, it was too late. Mr. Ellis, the man who had given me his life, at forty-eight-years old, was gone. He lay there, motionless.

That day was one of the worst of my life. I cried like never before; it was extremely difficult to accept that Mr. Ellis was gone. I was in disbelief, numb, and my world came to a sudden stop. What was I going to do without him? Who would I talk to when the world's problems were too heavy to bear? Who would I share life with? I was lost.

After hours of mourning, reality set in. I dreaded leaving for South Korea in a few days for another two-week tour. I had a long conversation with Johnette, Mr. Ellis's wife, in which I expressed my decision to cancel the tour and stay close to home with family. I told her there was no way I could do this tour; I was broken. We cried and we hugged. Then, as we walked down the cold, long hallway from Mr. Ellis's room, Johnette told me, "I understand and respect your decision, but you have to be strong and carry this commitment out. You are going! Because Mister wouldn't want you to cancel. Remember? No matter what, we never cancel because the show must go on!" I didn't want to hear it, but she was exactly right. That is what Mr. Ellis would have told me. Johnette closed the conversation by saying, *"Mister no longer lives beside you; he now lives within you."* I cried for hours after. Later, when I took a walk with my wife outside the hospital, I knew what I had to do. I asked for blessings from my family, packed, and continued with my scheduled tour.

The South Korea tour was one of the most successful I've ever done, but it was also one of the most difficult. Every single show, I had to leave my real-life emotions at the side of the stage and, as Mr. Ellis would say, "Put your Superman cape on," and perform my heart out. The day finally came when I did my last concert. I had one full day off in Seoul before heading back home.

As I looked out of my room at the amazing view of Seoul, I heard Mr. Ellis's voice: "I'm proud of you. You are stronger than you realize, and everything is going to be okay." Reality set in once again, but this time even stronger, because I knew when I got home, it would be for his funeral, and I was the one chosen to write and speak his eulogy. The journey home was long. All I did was emote and cry on the plane.

Mr. Ellis's passing made me feel like half of me had died. I was lost; he was the father figure I had always longed for. He was like my dad living through another person's body.

Mr. Ellis's funeral came and went, as did the holidays. I entered the new year knowing my life would be different. I was still numb, shocked, healing, and trying to find a way to move on from Mister's passing. I didn't want to do anything; I felt like a sandbag dragging out of bed. Every day was extremely difficult.

Then one morning, just a few months after Mr. Ellis's passing, I got a call from my dear friend Irene. She expressed her condolences and wanted to make sure I was in a good space, in mind, body, and spirit. I wasn't. She continued the conversation and, to my surprise, told me she was the curator for TEDx Santa Cruz. Their theme was "Activate." She invited me to talk about Mr. Ellis and how he had "activated" my life's journey through the ukulele. My immediate response was an absolute "No!" I initially thought, *How dare someone ask me to speak about Mr. Ellis, my best friend and father figure, who just died? I'm still hurt, lost, and looking for a way to move on and heal. I don't think I even mourned the loss entirely!* To some degree, I felt offended because I thought the world didn't understand me. So, I closed myself off from everyone and everything.

In all honesty, one of my ultimate dreams was to speak on a TEDx stage, but I surely didn't expect it to be about Mr. Ellis!

However, Irene kept calling me, insisting I take this opportunity. I kept declining. I didn't feel ready, especially to talk about Mr. Ellis.

Then one afternoon, right before picking up my boys from school, Irene called again. She asked if I was up to accepting the TEDx invitation. I said, "No, I don't think I am ready." There was silence, an awkward pause. I heard Irene take a deep breath and say in her stern but understanding voice, *"Listen, I get it. You're hurting and still healing, but being a TEDx speaker isn't about you; this is about Mr. Ellis! The world needs to hear Mister's story, and the only way that will happen is through you. Just you!"* I will never forget that conversation. It resonates with me every single day.

On March 8, 2014, a dream came true that was bigger than I ever envisioned. I not only became a speaker at TEDx Santa Cruz, but I also honored and shared the story of my best friend, *hanai* dad, and great mentor, Mr. Sam Ellis III.

Through the pain and the triumph, I learned that life is a series of seasons, each with its own challenges and joys. Embracing these seasons, this grief, accepting the changes, and finding strength in the journey is what truly defines us. It is the essence of navigating your life's griefs.

## WHAT I LEARNED

Life happens, and the seasons of life shape us. The ups, downs, and everything in between are beyond our control. All we can do is accept and embrace the moment. Initially, we may never understand the timing of things or the reasons behind them, but life happens for us to grow, gain appreciation, and seize opportunities.

Navigating your life's seasons means recognizing that each phase brings its own lessons and gifts. The highs teach us gratitude and joy, reminding us to savor every moment of happiness. The lows, though painful, are where we find our strength, resilience, and true character. They force us to dig deep, persevere, and emerge stronger than before.

Embracing the seasons of life means acknowledging that change is constant. It's about understanding every challenge is an opportunity in disguise, every setback a setup for a greater comeback. When we adopt this mindset, we start to see the beauty in life's unpredictability. We learn to trust the process, even when it doesn't make sense, and find peace in the journey itself.

By navigating your life's seasons and overcoming grief for loved ones, you allow yourself to be fully present. You learn to let go of the need for control and to accept that everything happens for a reason, even if the reason isn't immediately clear. This acceptance opens you up to new possibilities and allows you to grow in ways you never imagined.

So, navigate your life's seasons by squarely facing your grief with open arms. Trust that each moment, each experience, is part of your unique journey. Find the lessons, cherish the memories, and let every season shape you into the person you are meant to be.

**EXERCISE**

1. Coping with Difficult Times

   - Question: Have you ever experienced a time or loss so difficult it left you feeling paralyzed? How did you begin to cope and heal?

   - Activity: Write a letter to your past self during that difficult time describing your emotions, struggles, and the steps you took to start healing.

   - Reflection: How has your perspective on that time changed, and what lessons did you learn that you can apply to current or future challenges?

   _____

   _____

   _____

   _____

2. Adapting to Change

   - Question: How do you typically respond to change, and which strategies help you adapt to new seasons?

   - Activity: Create a personal change management plan outlining strategies you use or could use to adapt to change, such as mindfulness practices, seeking support, or setting new goals.

- Reflection: Reflect on a recent change you faced and how these strategies helped you navigate the transition.

_____

_____

_____

_____

3. Finding Strength in Adversity

- Question: Can you recall a time when you found unexpected strength during a difficult period? How did you overcome that challenge?

- Activity: Write a journal entry about a time when you discovered your inner strength, detailing the situation and your actions.

- Reflection: How did that experience change your perception of your capabilities, and how can you draw on this inner strength in future challenges?

_____

_____

_____

_____

4. Preserving Legacies and Learning from Loss

- Question: How do you preserve the memory of those who have influenced you, and how has loss shaped your personal growth?

- Activity: Create a tribute to someone who has significantly influenced your life. It could be a written story, a photo album, a video, or whatever medium appeals to you.

- Reflection: Reflect on how sharing their story shapes your understanding of their legacy and your own life. How does this practice help you stay connected to their memory and apply the lessons learned from loss?

_____

_____

_____

_____

## FIVE TIPS FOR NAVIGATING LIFE'S SEASONS AND OVERCOMING GRIEF

1. **Embrace Change and Acknowledge the Seasons of Life:** Recognize that life is comprised of various seasons, each with its own challenges and opportunities. Embrace change as a natural part of this cycle, understanding that growth often comes from navigating transitions.

2. **Find Strength in Adversity and Resilience Amid Loss:** Reflect on moments of adversity as opportunities to discover your inner strength.

Even in the face of profound loss, recognize the resilience that emerges when you confront grief head-on.

3. **Honor Legacy and Sharing Stories:** Consider the power of storytelling in preserving the memory and legacy of loved ones. By sharing the stories of those who have profoundly influenced your life, you can keep their spirit alive and inspire others.

4. **Embrace Growth and Learning from Loss:** Explore how moments of loss and grief can catalyze personal growth and transformation. Recognize the lessons and insights gained through navigating the seasons of life and how they activate your potential for growth.

5. **Cultivate Gratitude and Find Purpose:** Consider how challenges and setbacks can ultimately lead to opportunities for gratitude and personal fulfillment. By embracing the lessons learned from those who have influenced you and channeling them into positive action, you can cultivate a deeper sense of purpose and meaning.

## SUMMARY

Mr. Ellis's passing led me to realize life's journey is akin to climbing a mountain, with its peaks and valleys. Ultimately, his loss became a source of strength and perspective. It also helped me learn I have the power to shape my perception, viewing each experience as an opportunity for growth and acceptance. His belief in me, even during moments of self-doubt, continues to inspire, reminding me his legacy lives on within me. Through introspection, I recognized the need to embody strength and resilience, embracing each day as an opportunity for personal growth. Mr. Ellis instilled in me the understanding that life isn't merely a series of events happening to us but an unfolding narrative in which we play an active role.

Navigating grief and life's different seasons teaches us invaluable lessons. But knowledge alone isn't enough; we must apply these lessons to continue growing. In the next chapter, we'll see how applying life lessons has shaped my journey.

## CALL TO ACTION

I challenge you to navigate your life's seasons—the highs, the lows, and everything in between. Understand that amid the trials and tribulations are invaluable lessons waiting to be learned. Let the "Ls" in your life represent not losses, but lessons, guiding you toward a deeper understanding of yourself and the world around you. Embrace navigating your life's seasons with resilience and gratitude, knowing each phase contributes to growth and fulfillment.

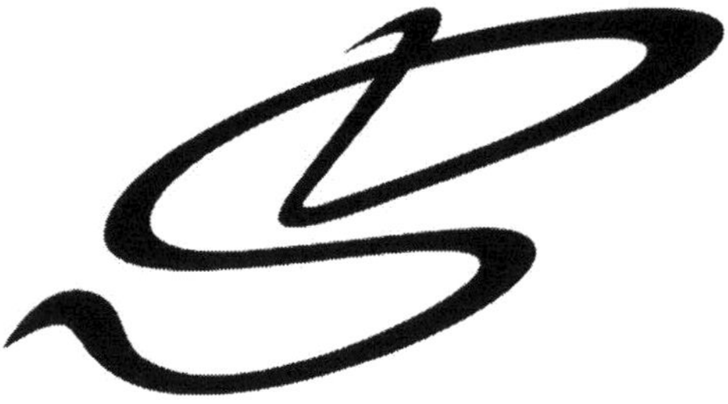

# SECTION 3:

# BUILDING YOUR INNER STRENGTH

"You gain strength, courage, and confidence by every experience in which you really stop to look fear in the face. You must do the thing you think you cannot do."

— Eleanor Roosevelt

# DOWNLOAD AND STREAM SONG FOR FREE!

www.DerickSebastian.com/WhatsGoingOn

# WHAT'S GOING ON?

Song Written and Performed by Derick Sebastian

What's going on with the world today?

There's so much trouble we the people got a lot to say

What's going on with the world today?

There's so much hurt we the people got to stop and pray

The hate, discrimination, racism, and stealing

This is what I'm fighting for. Injustice is what I'm feeling

I can't stop, won't stop. I can't give up, no!

I'll keep marching on 'till I reach the top, ya see

I'm slipping, I'm gripping, I can't breathe anymore

I'm punching underwater. It's a never-ending war

I stand strong to fight for what is right

It doesn't matter skin color, black, yellow, brown, red, or white

Now where is everybody who's supposed to be in charge?

They're pointing fingers, putting blame, just looking good and living large

They talk the talk but never walk the walk. They never stop

Their lack of actions speaks louder than words. Now here's my thought

I've got a voice, it's my heart to be heard

I'm here to make a difference, this is what I deserve, ya see

I'm speaking my mind, to find and help the blind

This is me, can't you see? I just wanna be free, yeah!

I wake up every day to do what is right and sacrifice

My blood sweat and tears are the only things that gratifies

You and me, eye to eye and unite, we're holding hands standing strong, fighting the good fight

Love over hate, faith over fear

Hope is all I got, but I'm far from near, ya see

This is our time, together we stand tall. Peace, love, and justice for all, yeah!

www.DerickSebastian.com

# CHAPTER 9

# TURNING YOUR ADVERSITY INTO OPPORTUNITY

"Do not judge me by my success,
judge me by how many times I fell down and got back up again."

— Nelson Mandela

Have you ever faced a challenge so overwhelming it felt impossible to overcome? How did you find the strength to move forward? When life throws unexpected obstacles your way, do you see them as roadblocks or steppingstones? What if the pain and setbacks you've experienced are actually the keys to unlocking your true potential? As you read on, consider how embracing adversity might reshape your journey and turn your greatest struggles into powerful opportunities for growth.

## MY STORY

In 2014, I was on a three-week ukulele tour in South Korea. The tour was a dream come true—sold-out shows, packed workshops, and a chance to share my passion for music with a new audience. Everything was going smoothly as I moved from city to city, but as the tour drew to a close, something unexpected happened. A sharp, irritating pain began to develop in my left ankle. It started as mild discomfort but quickly escalated, becoming so severe I could barely put any weight on it. This wasn't the result of an injury—I hadn't twisted or sprained my ankle, yet the pain was relentless.

The timing couldn't have been worse. I was gearing up for my final concert in Seoul, another big sold-out show. I didn't want to disappoint my fans or let the pain overshadow my performance. My tour manager, sensing my distress, provided me with some strong medication to help me push through the pain. With sheer determination, I managed to perform that night, but the pain lingered in the background, reminding me something was wrong.

After the tour, I sought medical help and underwent several tests. The diagnosis was a surprise—I had gout, a complex form of arthritis caused by an excess of uric acid in the blood. The acid crystalizes in the joints, causing intense pain, swelling, and inflammation. In my case, the gout attacks were centered in my left ankle. I was stunned. How could this be happening to me, especially when I was on such a high in my career?

In the years that followed, I made significant lifestyle changes to manage my condition. I became a vegetarian, cut out coffee and refined sugar, and focused on maintaining a healthy weight. These changes helped, and the gout attacks became less frequent. I thought I had it under control—until late 2020.

I was at one of Wailea's beautiful beaches, enjoying a peaceful walk along the shoreline, when I stepped into a small sand hole and mildly twisted my left ankle. It seemed like a minor incident, but it triggered the worst gout attack of my life. My ankle swelled to an alarming size, almost merging with my calf, and the pain was excruciating. I couldn't walk and was confined to crutches for months.

The pain was relentless. No medication seemed to help. My doctors tried everything—cortisone shots, steroids, painkillers—but nothing worked. For nearly seven months, I was trapped in a cycle of constant pain and frustration. I was doing everything right—eating clean, exercising, avoiding triggers—yet I was still suffering.

After months of research and consultations with specialists, I discovered my vegetarian diet, which I thought was helping, was actually contributing to my condition. Nightshade vegetables—tomatoes, potatoes, eggplant, and peppers—were triggering my gout attacks. I eliminated these foods from my diet, adjusted my medication, and gradually, the attacks became less frequent. I could finally walk again, then run, and eventually return to lifting weights.

This experience taught me profound lessons about resilience, adaptability, and the importance of listening to my body. It was a reminder that life is full of unexpected challenges, and how we respond to them shapes our journey. It reinforced the idea that setbacks are often opportunities in disguise—if we're willing to learn from them.

## WHAT I LEARNED

Life lessons surround us every day, both good and bad. It's up to us to learn from them. My experience with gout was a stark reminder that nothing is guaranteed. We must earn every success and embrace every challenge as an opportunity to grow.

In the past, I might have viewed this health crisis as a roadblock, something to overcome quickly so I could move on. But I've learned every challenge holds a lesson, and the key is to remain open to learning, even when the process is painful.

When faced with the reality of my condition, I realized it wasn't just about overcoming physical pain but about adapting my mindset and lifestyle to manage it effectively. The journey was difficult, but it taught me resilience, patience, and the importance of never giving up, even when the odds seem overwhelming.

This chapter of my life reminded me of the power of perspective. How we choose to view our challenges determines how we move through them. By shifting my focus from the pain to finding a solution, I regained control of my life. It wasn't easy, but it was necessary.

A football coach I know always preached, "If you want to win, you have to play hurt!" Life is like that. I had to perform my concert while "hurt." To achieve your best life, you too may have to "play hurt" at times. When you think about it, virtually everyone who has achieved massive success has often "played hurt" on their ascent to the top. It's certainly no fun, but it's better than the alternative—quitting, which is never an option for me. I encourage you never to let it become an option for you.

**EXERCISE**

1.  Embracing the Unexpected

    - Question: How do you typically react to unexpected challenges? Are you open to learning from them, or do you see them as setbacks?

    - Activity: Think of a recent unexpected challenge. Write down how you initially reacted and then list three potential lessons or opportunities that could come from the experience.

    - Reflection: How can shifting your perspective on unexpected challenges help you grow? What actions can you take to be more open to learning from such experiences in the future?

    _____

    _____

    _____

1.  Listening to Your Body

    - Question: How well do you listen to the signals your body sends you? Have you ignored those signals in some areas of your life to your detriment?

    - Activity: Reflect on a time when your body was trying to tell you something, whether through pain, fatigue, or discomfort. Write about how you responded and what the outcome was. Then, think about how you can better listen to your body going forward.

- Reflection: How might paying closer attention to your body's signals improve your overall well-being and resilience? What steps can you take to be more attuned to your physical health?

_____

_____

_____

_____

2. Reframing Health Challenges

- Question: When faced with a health challenge, how do you typically respond—do you fight it, ignore it, or embrace it as a part of your journey?

- Activity: Write about a health challenge you or someone close to you faced. Describe the emotions and thoughts that came with it, and then reframe the situation by identifying the lessons learned or the strength gained through that experience.

- Reflection: How can viewing health challenges as opportunities for growth change your approach to wellness? What positive habits can you adopt to better manage your health and well-being?

_____

_____

_____

_____

3.  Developing a Resilient Mindset

    *   Question: How resilient is your mindset when facing adversity? What strategies do you use to stay strong in difficult times?

    *   Activity: Create a "Resilience Plan" by identifying three strategies you can use to strengthen your mindset during tough times. Strategies could include mindfulness practices, physical activities, or reaching out for support. Write down how you will implement these strategies in your daily life.

    *   Reflection: How can developing a resilient mindset help you navigate life's challenges more effectively? What changes can you make today to build and maintain resilience?

    _____

    _____

    _____

    _____

## FIVE TIPS FOR TURNING YOUR ADVERSITY INTO OPPORTUNITY

1.  **Shift Your Perspective:** Instead of viewing challenges as obstacles, see them as opportunities to grow. Ask yourself, "What can I learn from this?" By changing your mindset, you can transform difficulties into valuable life lessons.

2. **Embrace Resilience:** Understand setbacks are a natural part of any journey. Cultivate resilience by remaining committed to your goals, even when things get tough. Remember, each time you bounce back, you become stronger and better equipped to handle future challenges.

3. **Adapt and Innovate:** When faced with adversity, be open to change and willing to adapt. Sometimes the path forward requires a new approach or a creative solution. Use challenges as a catalyst for innovation and personal growth.

4. **Seek Support and Guidance:** Don't be afraid to lean on others during tough times. Whether it's advice from a mentor, support from friends, or professional help, surrounding yourself with a strong support system can provide the strength and perspective needed to turn adversity into an opportunity.

5. **Stay Focused on Your Purpose:** Keep your long-term goals and purpose in mind, even when facing setbacks. By remaining focused on what truly matters, you can navigate adversity with a clear sense of direction, turning challenges into steppingstones toward your ultimate success.

## SUMMARY

In this chapter, we explored the transformative power of turning adversity into opportunity. Life is full of unexpected challenges, but how we choose to respond to them defines our journey. By shifting our perspective, embracing resilience, and staying focused on our purpose, we can navigate even the toughest times with strength and determination. We also discussed the importance of adapting to change and seeking support when needed, recognizing every setback is a potential setup for a comeback. Through these experiences, we not only grow stronger, but we gain valuable insights that can propel us toward greater achievements. Ultimately, this chapter reminds us that adversity, when approached with the right mindset, can be a powerful catalyst for growth and success.

## CALL TO ACTION

I challenge you to reflect on a recent adversity you've faced. Instead of seeing it as a setback, ask yourself how it could be an opportunity in disguise. What lessons can you extract from this experience? How can you use these insights to propel yourself forward? Take a moment to reframe your mindset—view challenges not as obstacles, but as steppingstones toward your growth and success. Start today by identifying one action you can take to turn adversity into an opportunity, and commit to making that change. Remember, the power to transform your journey lies within you. Embrace the challenge, and watch how it can reshape your life.

www.DerickSebastian.com

# CHAPTER 10

# FINDING YOUR WHY

"Family is not an important thing. It's everything."

— Michael J. Fox

**W**hat sacrifices are you willing to make for the people you love? How do you balance pursuing your dreams with responsibilities and commitments to your family? Can you navigate a life driven by both passion and purpose without losing sight of those who matter most? What happens when the demands of your journey pull you away from your loved ones? How do you stay connected through it all?

## MY STORY

In 1996, during my sophomore year in high school, my future wife, Raymi, and I started off as really good friends. Initially, I wasn't particularly attracted to her; it was more about easygoing companionship, just hanging out as friends. To be honest, as weird as it may sound, I was actually more interested in her friends, and Raymi played the "matchmaker." But through conversation and just being ourselves, I noticed her inner beauty, which became the true source of attraction. I could be myself with no judgment, speak my heart and struggles, and simply enjoy her company and laugh. Raymi became my best friend. That's when I knew I would love to share my life with her. Like Mr. Ellis always told me, "Always be friends first, because the real beauty comes from the heart."

On April 17, 1997, I officially started dating my best friend. It's been one heck of a journey. It's a beautiful thing to reflect on us starting out as high school sweethearts.

We certainly faced our challenges, especially dealing with long-distance relationships as our paths took us to separate colleges and post-graduate education. We both had our insecurities, temptations, family pressures, and expectations along the way. It was hard, but we weathered our storms and never gave up on each other.

Raymi and I eventually got married on December 19, 2004, and it was one of the best decisions I've ever made. It was a commitment not just to her but to God that I would be a faithful husband through thick and thin, 'til death do us part. We became one. And even though I didn't realize it back then, it was one of the biggest blessings in my life because it laid the foundation for what was to come.

In 2005, our first son, Santana, was born. Then our second son, Marley, was born in 2008. Finally, our youngest son, Jackson, was born in 2010.

Being young parents with really young kids wasn't easy, but it gave life a whole different meaning. My music career took on a new perspective. I had a sense of urgency to find my way and make it through this ukulele journey. It was a calling, a new purpose in life.

I had to follow my heart and pursue my music dreams. I needed to pave the way, be an inspiration through action, and show my boys, "You need to follow your heart and dreams and go after them. No matter what anyone says or thinks, you be you and do you. You have a gift, and it's your job to find it and share it. And you've got to believe in yourself even when no one else does. Know that you have a purpose. It's your job to fulfill that calling and purpose. And if Dad can do it, so can you."

We had an extremely young but very close-knit family. We did everything together, and I mean everything. Even our date nights were with our kids. Raymi and I mutually agreed if our boys couldn't be there or an event didn't allow kids, we wouldn't show up. No disrespect to anyone or anything, but we knew our shared time was invaluable.

In August 2006, I officially made my music career my full-time passion project. I knew deep down inside there would be mountains and valleys of challenges and sacrifices ahead, but I needed to lead by example. I promised myself no matter what, I would find my way. This became a non-negotiable internal driving force that led me to overflowing opportunities.

My ukulele journey gained momentum over the years and, ultimately, allowed me to start traveling around the world, sharing the gift of music. Touring different states and countries and meeting so many amazing human beings was one of the best things I've ever done, but it came with a huge sacrifice—being away from my wife and children.

The most difficult times were when I had to leave for music tours. The two things that always haunt me to this day are, first, when I had to leave. I would look back at my house, and my boys would be standing at the picture window, just tall enough to look out of it, crying for me. This tore my heart out because I knew if it was difficult for me, it was even more difficult for my wife and boys.

Second, it always disrupted my wife and boys' routine. My going back and forth, coming home and leaving year-round, was a double-edged sword. Consistency was a huge problem.

Leaving was already difficult, but while traveling, I'd try to call and check in. For the most part, because of my touring schedule and time differences, Raymi was at work, and the kids were either in school, busy with baseball practice, or already sleeping. We would mostly miss each other. If we were lucky enough to connect, it was always a quick surface talk. We all missed each other so much, but it was difficult to express our feelings to one another, especially with the inconsistencies in family time.

I was present at home. I was heavily involved in our boys' everyday routine, such as getting them up and ready for school, drop-offs, pick-ups, practices, cooking, cleaning, daycare, and everything in between. But when I had to leave, it was a shock to our family. There was a sudden gap, like "What do we do without Dad?" Raymi would be so stressed because not only did she have to take on my responsibilities on top of her own, but the boys would act out and give her a hard time because of my absence. Raymi became a single parent every time I left. It was a lot of strain on our family, especially for our boys.

When I'd finally come back, usually after at least a few weeks, it felt like Raymi and the boys didn't need me anymore. I slowly had to slide back into their routine, and I almost felt like they had to learn how to let their dad into their lives again.

It was extremely difficult. Raymi and I were always exhausted from our own work endeavors, plus taking care of the boys. Juggling it all was a struggle. We had many late nights and disagreements, but we had to compromise and find a way to make it work.

The answer? Our foundational faith in God.

Raymi is the biggest blessing in my life. She's the rock of our family. Even though my ukulele path has taken me away and stressed our family, she always rises above, trusts the process, and unconditionally supports my music journey. My success is her success; it's our family's success.

Family means everything to me. It's my *why*.

It is why I work so hard and never give up. It's why I can't fail. And it's why I always find a way to succeed in whatever I put my mind to.

In the midst of all this, one particular memory highlighting the sacrifices and my family's unwavering support stands out. I had to leave for a significant music tour. The night before my departure, Raymi and I stayed up late, packing my bags and preparing for the weeks ahead. A quiet understanding existed between us—unspoken but deeply felt—that we were in this together. As I finished packing, Raymi handed me a small, handwritten note. It was a simple message of love and encouragement, reminding me of why I was doing what I was doing. It read, *"We love you so much, and we're always proud of you. Go for your dream because it's our dream."* That note stayed with me throughout the tour, a constant reminder of my family's support and the driving force behind my pursuit.

Another vivid memory involves my boys. During one of my longer tours, I missed Santana's big baseball game. It was his first time pitching, and I knew how much it meant to him. We managed to video call just before the game. I gave him a pep talk, trying to be there for him despite the miles between us. Raymi recorded the game and sent it to me. Watching it alone in a hotel room, I felt a mix of pride and longing. Santana had done great, but I wished I could have been there in person. Those moments of absence were tough, but they also fueled my determination to make every second at home count.

Despite the challenges, sacrifices, and moments of doubt, what kept me going was the deep-seated belief that I was living out my purpose. Every performance, every tour, every interaction with fans was a testament to the journey Raymi and I had embarked on together. Our shared sacrifices weren't just for me; they were for us, for our family, and for the legacy we were building.

I've got one shot to honor my family. That's my true motivation—finding our *why*.

**WHAT I LEARNED**

My family had to come first, not my music. When I prioritized my music above all else, things just didn't align. But when I put my family first, it gave a whole new meaning and purpose to what I was going after. The true meaning of success wasn't in my music—it was in my family.

This realization shifted my entire perspective. I understood my family's well-being and happiness were the real indicators of my success. Music was a passion and a calling, but it was my family that grounded me and gave me the strength to pursue my dreams. When I focused on nurturing my family, everything else began to fall into place. The support, love, and joy we shared became the foundation upon which I built my career.

Family doesn't have to be just blood relations. It's about cultivating great relationships filled with love and laughter. If you surround yourself with people who genuinely care for you, who uplift and support you, they become your family. This sense of belonging and connectedness brings a profound sense of calmness and joy.

I've learned that success is not measured by accolades or achievements but by the quality of relationships and the love we share with others. When I prioritize my family—whether it's my wife and kids or the extended family of friends and mentors who support me—I find the strength and inspiration to keep pushing forward. They are my anchor, my reason, my *why*.

Having a supportive family, whether by blood or by bond, means having a sanctuary where you can be yourself, where you are understood and appreciated. This support is crucial, especially when facing the ups and downs of pursuing a dream. It provides a safe space to recharge, reflect, and refocus.

In moments of doubt or when the challenges seemed overwhelming, my family's love and encouragement kept me going. Knowing they believed in me, even when I struggled to believe in myself, made all the difference. Their faith in my abilities fueled my perseverance and determination.

This lesson has been invaluable. By putting my family first, I've found a deeper, more fulfilling purpose in everything I do. My music career became not just about personal success but about creating a legacy honoring and supporting my family. This alignment between my personal and professional life has brought me a sense of peace and fulfillment I never thought possible.

As you navigate your own journey, remember to prioritize the relationships that matter most. Surround yourself with people who love and support you, and let their presence be your guiding light. When you focus on building and nurturing these connections, you'll find everything else begins to align. Success will come not just from what you achieve but from the love and joy you cultivate along the way.

**EXERCISE**

1.  Reflecting on Family's Role

    - Question: How does your family's unconditional love shape your life? What role have they played in bringing out the best in you?

    - Activity: Create a "Family Effect" journal to document specific instances where your family's support helped you overcome challenges or achieve goals.

    - Reflection: How does recognizing these moments affect your current perspective on the importance of family?

_____

_____

_____

_____

_____

_____

_____

_____

_____

_____

_____

_____

2. Balancing Ambitions and Relationships

- Question: How do you balance your personal ambitions with your family or other significant relationships? Do some areas need adjustment?

- Activity: Create a balance chart listing your personal ambitions on one side and your family commitments on the other. Identify areas of imbalance.

- Reflection: What specific steps can you take to create a more balanced life that honors both your ambitions and your relationships?

_____

_____

_____

_____

_____

3. Defining Success Beyond Achievements

- Question: How do you define success? Could including relational achievements shift your approach to achieving your goals?

- Activity: Redefine your success criteria to include both personal and relational achievements. Write a new definition of success that aligns with this perspective.

- Reflection: How does this expanded definition of success change your priorities and daily actions? What new goals will you set based on this broader perspective?

_____

_____

_____

_____

4.  Leveraging Support

- Question: How has your faith or support system helped you through tough times? How can you strengthen this foundation moving forward?

- Activity: Reflect on a difficult time and write a detailed account of how your faith or support system helped you navigate it.

- Reflection: What practices can you incorporate to maintain and build upon this support system, ensuring it continues to help you through future challenges?

_____

_____

_____

_____

_____

## FIVE TIPS FOR FINDING YOUR *WHY*

1.  **Recognize the Influence of Relationships:** Reflect on the relationships that shaped your life. Identify how connections with others have influenced your sense of purpose and direction.

2.  **Embrace the Power of Commitment:** Understand the importance of commitment. Whether it's to a partner, family, or a cause, recognize how committing to something greater than yourself can become your *why*.

3. **Balance Personal Ambitions with Core Values:** Identify your passions and career goals, but also consider what truly grounds you. Balancing personal ambitions with your core values helps align your priorities and leads to a more fulfilling life.

4. **Draw Strength from Faith and Support:** Consider the role of faith and support in your life. Whether through spiritual beliefs or the encouragement of loved ones, these elements can provide strength and motivation to pursue your dreams.

5. **Redefine Success Through Relationships:** Reflect on what success means to you. Understand that true success is often not just about individual achievements but about the happiness and well-being of those around you.

## SUMMARY

By sharing my journey with my wife Raymi, including our challenges and the joy of raising our three sons, I discovered that while pursuing a career in music provided me with a sense of accomplishment, the true foundation of my happiness and drive was my family. Marrying Raymi and becoming a father didn't just enrich my life; it redefined my understanding of success.

This revelation showed me my ultimate *why* wasn't individual accolades but the shared moments and deep connections with my family. Supported by unwavering faith in God and encouragement from mentors, I learned life's true purpose is less about personal achievement and more about the relationships we cherish and nurture. This is the essence of finding your *why*.

Knowing your *why* provides motivation, especially during dark times. Facing and surviving these moments are crucial to your journey. Next, let's explore how to navigate the darkest times.

## CALL TO ACTION

I challenge you to reflect on the foundations of your motivations. What or who really drives you to succeed? Think about whether your current priorities align with these deeper motivations. How might your life change if you align your daily actions with your true *why*? Consider making one small change this week to better integrate your fundamental motivations into your daily life.

www.DerickSebastian.com

# CHAPTER 11

# SURVIVING YOUR DARK TIMES

"Tough times never last, but tough people do."

— Robert H. Schuller

H ave you ever faced a time when everything felt like it was falling apart? How do you find the strength to keep going when the weight of the world is on your shoulders? What happens when your dreams seem to be slipping away and you start to question your purpose? How do you navigate the darkest times and find the courage to keep fighting?

## MY STORY

The journey that is my musical adventure has been nothing short of a rollercoaster ride. Sometimes it was easy enough to handle, but most times, it wasn't.

In 2009, I hustled every day, trying to find my way. Getting up early before the family, I planned new ways to expand in the local music scene and somehow tap into corporate performances. Our second son, Marley, had just been born, and we had just moved into a bigger home. These were exciting times. Our family was growing, but so were our expenses.

I was not prepared for what lay ahead.

Shortly after this new chapter with my growing family began, the world's economy took a turn for the worse. The recession hit hard. Everything was tanking. Most of my gigs were still low-paying, but they were all I really had—no other income. It was pretty scary—two mortgages (because we kept and rented out our first home while living in the second), loans, credit card bills, utility bills, and a family to provide for.

In 2010, our third son, Jackson, was born. By then, life was chaotic in too many ways. I had three young boys, a wife trying to do her part, a music career I was chasing, and bills everywhere. Our finances were out of control; the struggle was real.

I found myself more depressed every day. I lost a lot of weight. I was getting sick more often. Everything felt like it was going downhill.

We didn't have much money to spare. We were scraping the bottom of the barrel every month. The pressure to be strong and raise my young family was the worst feeling. There I was, trying to make it as a full-time music artist, but nothing was working. Things didn't look good. They surely didn't feel good either. I was lost and living in regret. Had I made the right choice going after my music dream? Had I been naive when I thought I could handle the stress? Was the dream too big to handle? What the hell had I been thinking, risking it all—even my family? Maybe I should have taken a different career path.

I felt like a complete failure. I wanted to run away from the heaviness of my everyday problems. I didn't know what to do, where to go, or even what to say. My life was spiraling. It became dark. The urge to just give up became stronger every day.

I became depressed. Thoughts of ending my life were knocking on my front door. I felt I wasn't good enough. I wasn't worth my place on earth. My wife and boys deserved better. I could end the misery by taking one drastic step. Life was dark, scary, and uncertain.

The pressure of trying to make it in my music career, be a faithful husband and father, and somehow be financially stable was just too much. I didn't think I could provide for my family.

I felt like I was living a different life, and the world didn't see it—or at least I didn't let the world see it. Maybe it would just be better if I wasn't here and could be with my dad. But would my dad really want that for me? I lost hope. I lost my faith in God.

Throughout the years that followed, life was a series of relentless ups and downs. I found myself trapped in cycles of darkness, where no matter how hard I worked or how much I tried, nothing seemed to go right. The weight of mounting debt and ever-increasing bills felt like a crushing burden.

During the darkest times, when I was battling temporary bouts of depression, thoughts of suicide surfaced. The idea of ending my pain seemed like a way out. But my strong faith in God and deep love for my wife and children kept me from ever acting on those thoughts. I knew I could never leave my children in the same situation I had faced as a child: growing up without a father.

I understood these struggles were part of the process of succeeding as a musician, artist, and entrepreneur. I knew I had to battle through the darkness, work even harder, and continue developing my skills. With God's grace, I believed things would get better—and they did. Eventually, my life and business flourished beyond what I could have imagined.

If you, or anyone you know, has ever had similar thoughts of escaping your problems by giving up on life itself, I urge you to seek help. Suicide doesn't eliminate your pain; it transfers it to your loved ones, leaving them to carry the burden for a lifetime.

How did I find my way out? God showed up for me, guiding me toward the light. No matter how deep the darkness was, I could always hear a faint voice saying, "Everything is going to be okay. Just keep trusting me. Be still, and know that I am God."

I fought to live. I fought to win life every day. I fought to live in joy and be grateful in the moment despite my circumstances. I made it an everyday mantra to live in faith over fear.

I started going to church to seek God's Word and message evermore—God's purpose for me. I started relying heavily on a local Maui weekly men's Bible group called MOI (Men of Integrity).

I eventually found the strength and courage to speak up and start talking about my depression and self-pity. More and more, God's word became stronger and played a bigger and bigger role in my everyday faith.

Life is a spiritual battle. At any given moment, if you are not strong in your faith, negative energy is ready to pounce! My struggles are still real. I still get down on myself more often than is healthy, but now I have a deeper perspective, a stronger purpose, and a solid foundation in God.

I realized my life on earth is temporary, and while I'm here I need to fulfill God's plan, not mine. This understanding has helped me through the hard times: It's not about me; it's about God and the purpose God gave me to fulfill here on earth. This realization gave me strength, enabling me to navigate and ultimately survive my dark times.

## WHAT I LEARNED

No matter how hard life gets, you cannot let yourself play the victim and feel sorry for yourself. Life doesn't happen to you; life happens for you. Every struggle, every setback, and every dark moment is a part of your journey, shaping you into who you are meant to be.

I learned embracing this mindset is crucial. It's easy to fall into the trap of self-pity, to look at the challenges and say, "Why me?" But I realized every hardship I faced was an opportunity to grow, a chance to build resilience and character. Instead of asking, "Why is this happening to me?" I started asking, "What is this teaching me?"

One of the most profound lessons I learned is how important perspective is. In the midst of your darkest times, it can feel like the world is closing in on you. But stepping back and looking at the bigger picture helps you see those moments are just a small part of the much bigger, beautiful tapestry of your life. Each thread, no matter how dark, contributes to the overall masterpiece.

I also learned the power of faith and trust. Trusting in God's plan, even when I couldn't see the light at the end of the tunnel, gave me the strength to keep moving forward. It reminded me my pain and struggles had a purpose. Trusting that everything happens for a reason, even if that reason is not immediately clear, helped me find peace in the chaos.

Another key lesson was about how important it is to have support. I found solace in my family, my church, and MOI. They provided a safe space for me to express my fears and frustrations, to cry and to heal. Their unwavering support reminded me I was not alone in my struggles. Surrounding yourself with people who uplift and encourage you is vital, especially during your darkest times.

Moreover, I discovered the significance of self-compassion. It's easy to be hard on myself, to criticize every mistake and regret every decision. But learning to forgive myself and be gentle with my soul was transformative. It allowed me to acknowledge my humanity and understand that perfection is not the goal—progress is.

Finally, I learned strength comes from within. External circumstances will always be unpredictable and often uncontrollable, but the strength to endure and overcome comes from deep inside. It's the quiet, persistent voice that says, "Keep going. You are stronger than you think." This inner strength ultimately guided me through surviving my dark times.

**EXERCISE**

1.  Reflecting on Your Darkest Hour

    *   Question: What was your darkest hour, and how did it shape your perspective on resilience and inner strength?

    *   Activity: Write a detailed account of this time, focusing on your emotions, thoughts, and the events that transpired.

    *   Reflection: What did you learn about your inner strength from this experience, and how can you apply these lessons to future challenges?

    _____

    _____

    _____

    _____

    _____

    _____

    _____

    _____

    _____

    _____

    _____

2. The Role of Support Systems

- Question: How has seeking support during difficult times changed your journey?

- Activity: List the people or groups you reached out to for support and describe how they helped you recover and grow.

- Reflection: How did these relationships change your experience, and what role do they continue to play?

_____

_____

_____

_____

_____

_____

3. Faith and Spirituality in Challenging Moments

- Question: How has faith or spirituality helped you navigate challenging moments?

- Activity: Reflect on specific instances where your faith provided comfort and strength, and write about their influence on your journey.

- Reflection: How does your faith continue to guide you, and what practices strengthen your spiritual resilience?

_____

_____

_____

_____

_____

_____

4.  Building and Maintaining Resilience

- Question: How do you cultivate resilience, and what strategies help you bounce back from setbacks?

- Activity: Create a resilience toolkit by identifying your top resilience-building strategies and how you can apply them in tough times.

- Reflection: How effective are these strategies in helping you cope, and what new practices can you explore to enhance your resilience?

_____

_____

_____

_____

_____

**FIVE TIPS FOR SURVIVING YOUR DARK TIMES**

1.  **Seek Support and Guidance:** In times of darkness, it's crucial to reach out to trusted friends, family members, or professionals for support. Surround yourself with people who uplift and encourage you, guiding you through the challenges you face.

2.  **Find Strength in Faith:** Whether it's through prayer, meditation, or seeking spiritual guidance, finding strength in faith can provide solace and hope during the darkest of times. Trusting in a Higher Power and surrendering to divine guidance can offer a sense of peace and purpose.

3.  **Practice Self-Compassion:** During times of struggle, it's easy to be hard on yourself and succumb to feelings of guilt or inadequacy. Practicing self-compassion involves treating yourself with kindness, understanding, and forgiveness. Recognize that it's okay to have difficult emotions and allow yourself the space to heal.

4.  **Focus on Learning and Growth:** Instead of viewing challenges as setbacks, see them as opportunities for growth and development. Embrace the lessons that come with adversity, knowing each trial offers a chance to learn, evolve, and emerge stronger than before.

5.  **Embrace Resilience:** Resilience is the ability to bounce back from adversity, to persevere in the face of challenges, and to remain steadfast in pursuit of your goals. Cultivate resilience by maintaining a positive outlook, adapting to change, and believing in your ability to overcome obstacles.

## SUMMARY

Life isn't easy, especially when faced with challenges that test your resolve and push you into the depths of uncertainty. However, these dark moments help you discover your spirit's true strength. Just as hard times don't last forever, neither do the feelings of despair or hopelessness. By embracing positivity, resilience, and a willingness to learn, you can navigate adversity and emerge stronger on the other side. By seeking support, finding strength in faith, practicing self-compassion, focusing on learning and growth, and embracing resilience, you can navigate even the toughest times with courage and grace. Life's trials have the power to shape us into stronger, wiser, and more compassionate people. The darkness doesn't last forever, but the lessons you learn and the strength you gain will endure. Embrace the journey, knowing you have the power within to overcome any obstacle that comes your way.

Surviving dark times often involves facing rejection and learning to forgive. These experiences can redirect us toward better paths. In the next chapter, we'll see how forgiveness and redirection played a role in my story.

## CALL TO ACTION

I challenge you to take some time to reflect on a difficult time and consider how it shaped you into the person you are today. Embrace the lessons learned from your dark moments and use them to cultivate resilience and strength as you face future challenges. This is a key to surviving your darkest times.

www.DerickSebastian.com

## CHAPTER 12

# KNOWING REJECTION IS YOUR REDIRECTION

"Often people just don't see what I see. They have too much doubt. You can't do your best when you're doubting yourself. If you don't believe in yourself, who will?"

— Michael Jordan

Have you ever faced doubt from those closest to you? How do you handle the sting of rejection and the weight of others' negative opinions? What happens when the people who should support you instead tell you your dreams are impossible? How do you find the strength to keep going, even when others don't believe in you?

## MY STORY

Throughout my crazy creative adventure, no matter how exciting things got, I always encountered doubters and sometimes haters.

When I first started playing the ukulele, I used to get teased by my classmates and even some baseball teammates. They said the ukulele was for "scrubs" and "wannabes." Even some of my immediate family said hurtful, doubting words in the beginning. Granted, at the time, the ukulele wasn't a popular instrument worldwide; it was seen as toy-like instrument. I've heard some say, "Derick thinks he's all that just because he can play the ukulele," or "He just wants attention." While I may not have heard it directly, what people said always circled back to me.

I was hurt badly inside because I had never done anything to anyone. I was not outspoken in school. I was more of an introvert who kept pretty quiet. I was respectful and totally enjoyed being around good vibes.

One of my worst experiences was hearing a family member tell me, "You can never make a living just playing your ukulele, so you need to find something else to do or a job that is more guaranteed, stable, and consistent."

I was hurt, confused, and most of all, angry. Why? Because I thought family was supposed to be supportive, unconditionally. The truth is it's not always that way. I knew what he was telling me wasn't true. But all I felt was doubt, not support. I remember losing sleep because I was so bothered by so many mixed feelings.

It was hard enough when I called venues to play at—such as restaurants, hotels, events, booking agencies, and destination management companies—

and I was told, "No. I'm sorry; what you're doing is not something we're looking for." I needed my family to back me up.

Yes, I often questioned myself when others doubted me. *Maybe I'm not on the right path*, I thought. But deep down inside, I truly believed I could somehow, someway, make a living playing my ukulele. I knew I could do this!

The doubt and rejection were tough. I could have given up many times along the way, but two sayings kept me going:

"Rejection is redirection."

— Tony Robbins

"Tough times don't last, but tough people do."

— Robert H. Schuller

These words of wisdom reminded me to see every setback as a new opportunity and to remain resilient through the challenges. When people doubt or talk down to you, it's nothing personal. It's really about what they are going through.

Let's face it; we all doubt ourselves at one time or another. We have the imposter syndrome, the feeling we're not good enough. But it is even worse when someone close doubts us—whether it's a friend, sibling, parent, relative, or just a close friend. It's tough because if we hear it consistently enough, our subconscious starts to believe these untrue things about ourselves.

We may want to point fingers and blame others (or perhaps we already did) for what happened in our life, but at the end of the day, blaming others just does one thing: hardens our heart. It makes us accept the burden while carrying the weight of other people's problems, which we really have no control over. We can't do anything or change others' opinions. But we can learn from them, even if they are being negative. Not using these lessons to better ourselves hinders our development and character. And our character is our true foundation.

Understanding this was crucial for my growth. I realized people's negative comments and doubts were more about their insecurities and limitations than my capabilities. By internalizing this insight, I started to let go of the resentment and focus on proving to myself, not others, I could achieve my dreams.

Sometimes the rejection was overwhelming. Each no from a venue or booking agent was like a blow to my confidence. It's easy to let those moments define you and make you question your path. But instead of seeing rejection as a final verdict on my abilities, I started seeing it as a redirection. Each rejection was steering me toward a better opportunity, a different path I might have missed otherwise.

This mindset shift didn't happen overnight. It took constant reflection and a deliberate effort to focus on the positive aspects of my journey. I reminded myself of the small victories and milestones along the way. Every successful gig, every appreciative audience, and every new opportunity became a testament to my resilience and determination.

Forgiving those who doubted me was a significant part of this journey. Holding onto anger and resentment only weighed me down. Forgiveness allowed me to free up mental and emotional space to concentrate on my goals. It wasn't about excusing their behavior; it was about liberating myself from the negativity that held me back.

In the face of doubt and rejection, I found strength in my passion for music and my unwavering belief in my potential. I surrounded myself with supportive people who believed in me and my vision. Their encouragement helped me remain focused and motivated, reinforcing the idea that I was on the right path.

Learning to forgive those who doubted me and understanding rejection was just a redirection was pivotal in my journey. It allowed me to focus on my path without carrying unnecessary emotional baggage. Seeing rejection as a detour rather than a dead end helped me navigate toward better opportunities and stay true to my dreams.

Remember, in your own journey, forgive those who doubt you; it frees you to keep moving forward.

**WHAT I LEARNED**

Believing in yourself is all that matters. People are going to talk, doubt, and have their own opinions, but the truth is, it's just noise distracting you from becoming the best version of yourself.

You will encounter naysayers and critics. Their words can sting, and their doubts can make you question your own worth. But it's crucial to understand their opinions are just that—opinions. They do not define you or your potential. Everyone has their own fears and insecurities, and sometimes, they project them onto you. Recognize this noise for what it is: a reflection of their limitations, not yours.

Believing in yourself requires tuning out the noise and focusing on your inner voice. This voice knows your dreams, your capabilities, and your passions. It's the voice that urges you to keep going when the world seems against you. Nurture this voice with positive affirmations and reminders of your achievements. Celebrate progress, no matter how small, and let these successes fuel your confidence.

One of the most powerful ways to build self-belief is to set small, achievable goals. Each time you accomplish one of these goals, you prove to yourself you are capable. These small victories accumulate over time, creating a solid foundation of confidence that is hard to shake. When faced with negativity or doubt from others, you can draw on these successes as evidence of your abilities.

Surrounding yourself with positive influences is also essential. Seek out those who support and uplift you, who believe in your vision and encourage your growth. Their positive energy will help reinforce your belief in yourself, creating a buffer against negativity. Remember, you have the power to choose who you let into your inner circle.

It's also important to understand that self-belief doesn't mean arrogance or ignoring constructive criticism. It's about having a balanced perspective, where you value your own opinion of yourself above others' unfounded doubts. Take in feedback that helps you grow, but discard the rest. Use criticism as a tool for improvement, not as a weapon to undermine your self-worth.

When you truly believe in yourself, you become unstoppable. This belief propels you forward, helps you overcome obstacles, and keeps you resilient in the face of challenges. It becomes your shield against the noise of doubt and negativity, allowing you to remain focused on your goals and aspirations.

Believing in yourself is the foundation of your journey. It is the cornerstone of your success and the key to unlocking your full potential. As you continue to pursue your dreams, let this belief be your guiding light, illuminating the path ahead and leading you toward the best version of yourself.

In the end, what truly matters is your unwavering confidence in your abilities and your commitment to your goals. Others may doubt, criticize, and try to bring you down, but believing in yourself will always lift you higher.

**EXERCISE**

1. What do you need to do to forgive others who have doubted, hated, or rejected you?

    • Activity: Write a letter to someone who doubted or rejected you, expressing your feelings honestly. Then, write another letter forgiving them. You don't have to send these letters; the act of writing can be therapeutic.

- Reflection: How does writing these letters change your perspective on forgiveness? What emotions surfaced during this process?

_____

_____

_____

_____

2. Reflect on a recent rejection. How can you view it as redirection to something potentially better for you?

- Activity: Write about a recent rejection and list possible new directions or opportunities it might open for you.

- Reflection: How does reframing the rejection as redirection motivate you and improve your outlook? What positive steps can you take next?

_____

_____

_____

_____

3.  Which affirmations can you use to reinforce self-belief when facing doubt from others?

    •   Activity: Create a list of positive affirmations that resonate with you. Place them where you can see them daily, such as on your mirror or phone screen.

    •   Reflection: How do these affirmations make you feel? Do they help counteract negativity from others? How can you incorporate them into your daily routine?

    _____

    _____

    _____

4.  Can you think of a time when criticism was more about the critic's personal struggles than about you? How can recognizing this help you forgive them?

    •   Activity: Reflect on a specific criticism and write about the possible personal struggles the critic might have been facing.

    •   Reflection: How does understanding their struggles change your feelings toward the criticism? Can you find empathy for their situation?

    _____

    _____

    _____

## FIVE TIPS FOR KNOWING REJECTION IS YOUR REDIRECTION

1.  **Recognize the Source of Criticism:** Understanding that criticism often stems from the critic's own issues can help you separate their negativity from your self-worth.

2.  **Reframe Rejection as Redirection:** This mindset can transform painful rejections into opportunities for growth and reveal new paths.

3.  **Build Resilience Against Doubt:** By affirming your self-belief and understanding that tough times are temporary, you strengthen your resilience.

4.  **Release the Burden of Blame:** Holding onto blame can be heavy and counterproductive. Forgiving others lightens this burden, allowing you to focus on your own growth.

5.  **Develop Character Through Challenges:** Every challenge and every doubt you face can be a steppingstone to building stronger character. Forgiveness is integral in using these experiences positively.

## SUMMARY

In this chapter, I explored the challenges of facing doubt, hate, and rejection while pursuing my dreams in music. Throughout my journey, from being teased about playing the ukulele to facing disbelief from family and frequent rejections from venues, I've encountered significant negativity. However, I've learned criticism often reflects the critic's personal struggles rather than my shortcomings. I've embraced the mantra "rejection is redirection" and realized tough times are simply part of the process of building resilience and character.

By choosing to forgive those who doubted or rejected me, I've freed myself from the burden of blame and negativity, allowing myself to focus on growth and continue striving toward becoming the best version of myself. This chapter underscored the power of forgiveness and emphasizes that, ultimately, believing in yourself is what truly matters. When you master this concept, you, too, will be free to turn your passion into your profession.

Rejection and forgiveness help us see our true selves more clearly. Recognizing and embracing our true colors is a powerful step toward personal growth. Next, let's explore this journey together.

## CALL TO ACTION

I challenge you to reflect on your own experiences with doubt and rejection. Is there someone you need to forgive to move forward more freely? Think about how holding onto resentment might be holding you back, and consider what letting go could do for your personal growth and happiness. How can you start the process of forgiving today to empower yourself and enhance your journey?

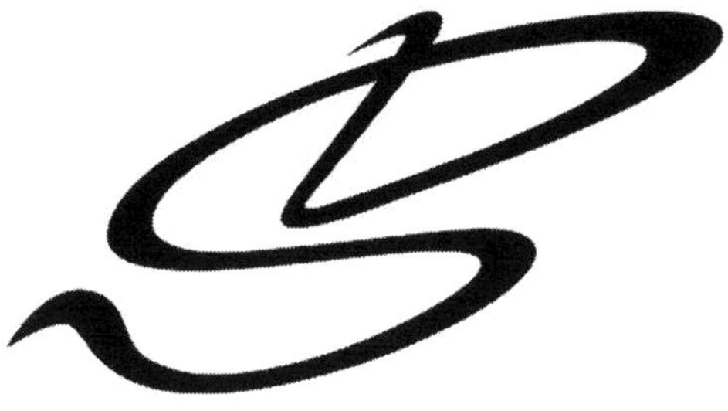

# SECTION 4:

# ACHIEVING YOUR PERSONAL GROWTH

"What lies behind us and what lies before us are tiny matters compared to what lies within us."

— Ralph Waldo Emerson

# DOWNLOAD AND STREAM SONG FOR FREE!

www.DerickSebastian.com/ItsTheLove

# IT'S THE LOVE

Song Written and Performed by Derick Sebastian

I'm watching the moonlight shine

Getting lost in the midnight sky

I'm keeping warm with my valentine


It's not hard for a girl like you

Who takes away all my lasting blues

I hope you feel the same way too


It's the love that I'm feeling

It's my heart that you're stealing

It's the love that I'm feeling

It's the love


It's the love that I'm feeling

Baby it's you that I'm falling for

It's the love that I'm feeling

It's the love

It's only you that makes me fly so high

I can't hide it, and I won't deny

Oh, I'm in love with my valentine


Here's my ring; will you marry me?

White doves, wedding bells by the sea

We'll dream away and start a family

www.DerickSebastian.com

www.DerickSebastian.com

# CHAPTER 13

# SEEING YOUR TRUE COLORS

"An optimist is a person who sees green light everywhere, while a pessimist sees only the red stoplight…the truly wise person is colorblind."

— Albert Schweitzer

H ave you ever felt different or hidden a part of yourself because you were afraid of what others might think? How do you handle the challenges that come with embracing your uniqueness? Have you ever faced a moment when you had to confront and accept a personal imperfection?

**MY STORY**

I was in kindergarten when a classmate asked, "Hey, can I please borrow your blue crayon?" Without hesitation, I said yes and popped open my box to get the blue crayon. But to my surprise, I couldn't tell the difference between the blues and purples. I quickly gathered all the dark colors in one hand and started reading the labels. When I found "blue," I quickly tossed it over and acted like nothing was wrong, but deep down, I knew something wasn't right.

I eventually realized I also couldn't tell the difference between the bright yellows and greens or the dark browns and reds.

It was the strangest thing. I didn't understand why, but I knew I was colorblind. As a shy, introverted kindergartener, I couldn't help but keep this secret weirdness to myself.

I was so embarrassed about being unable to tell the difference in colors that I found other cool ways to quickly identify them. I would rip off all the color labels of the blues and put them in one corner of my crayon box, then leave all the labels on the purples and put them in the opposite corner. I did the same with the yellows, greens, reds, and browns. Soon, the blues, yellows, and reds were label-less while the purples, browns, and greens had their labels left on. It was absolutely organized genius!

As elementary school went on, I found creative ways to adapt to my colorblindness. I relied on patterns, shapes, and context clues to determine colors. For example, I remembered the sky was always blue, so anything that looked like the sky must be blue. Grass was green, and the sun was yellow. These little tricks helped me navigate the world of colors, even though I still felt embarrassed about my condition.

Fast forward to the second grade. When I found out we would have physical tests, including a color test, I freaked out. I was nervous because I knew I had a vision problem I'd been hiding.

I passed the reading test and vision test, but then came the color test. I knew I was doomed. My teacher opened the color test book and asked, "What number do you see?"

"What number?"

She looked a little puzzled, turned to another page, and asked again, "What number do you see now?"

I didn't see a number—all I saw were dots all over the page. So, again, I said, "What number?"

My teacher skipped several pages and then asked, "What letter do you see?"

I couldn't see any letters either. I was so embarrassed because I knew she knew, and we both had to come to an accord. She quietly whispered, "I think you're colorblind, but we need to send you to the doctor's office to confirm."

I wanted to run away and lock myself in a room.

I was terrified. I was embarrassed. What would I tell my mom? I couldn't see colors. What would my siblings and friends think of me? That was one of the worst days of my life.

When Mom got the letter from the school, I was surprised she didn't make a big deal of it. We went to the doctor, went through all the testing, and sure enough, I couldn't tell the difference between blues, purples, browns, reds, and light green to yellow.

I was officially diagnosed as colorblind, even though technically I am really color deficient since I can see some colors.

For many years, I kept it a secret because I was so embarrassed about it. I didn't know anyone who was colorblind—probably because I was never open enough to talk about it. I felt a pang of anxiety every time we had a coloring activity in school. I would carefully watch my classmates to see what colors they used and try to mimic them. Sometimes, I even asked to borrow their crayons, just to be sure I was using the right color.

In one particular instance, I knew I had to accept my personal imperfection. In college, I took a prerequisite art class and had the absolutely hardest time. We dealt with colors every day, which was like pulling teeth for me. I was so stressed out. I dreaded that class. But no matter what, I kept my weirdness a secret because, in my mind, no one else was colorblind, only me.

One day, the professor asked us to create a color wheel, mixing primary colors to form secondary colors. I struggled immensely, and it was obvious to everyone something was off. The professor noticed my difficulty and asked me to stay after class. I felt the same dread I had felt back in second grade.

When I explained my color blindness, the professor was surprisingly understanding. She told me about famous artists who were also colorblind and how they had adapted their techniques. She encouraged me to embrace my unique perspective and use it to my advantage in my artwork.

It was a miracle—I passed with a "D." Was that even a passing grade?

Growing up, being colorblind was one of my biggest insecurities. It often made me feel inadequate and was an immense challenge to overcome. But I knew I had to let go of those negative feelings and embrace the person

God made me. Some things are beyond our control, and this was one of them. Over time, I learned to embrace my uniqueness and find strength in seeing the world through my own perspective.

All these years later, I am, of course, still colorblind. But I had a choice: I could let it hold me back, or I could use it as fuel to push myself even harder. I chose to use it to help motivate me to attain my dreams.

## WHAT I LEARNED

The weight I carried for years about being colorblind was simply unnecessary, but it taught me a big lesson and gave me permission to accept my perfect imperfection. You don't have to see all the colors to see true beauty. I realized the most meaningful things are still meaningful in black and white.

Being colorblind isn't really about not seeing colors; it's about having perspective. I may not be able to see the physical color of things, but I can see the true colors of life. This experience taught me to look beyond the surface and appreciate the deeper essence of everything around me. It's not about the hues and shades; it's about understanding, empathy, and the unique view that comes from embracing who you truly are. Through this lens, I've learned the true colors of life are revealed in the way we see and appreciate the world, no matter what our eyes can or cannot perceive.

**EXERCISE**

1. How do you accept your imperfections and embrace them as part of who you are?

   - Activity: Write a letter to yourself acknowledging your imperfections and expressing acceptance.

   - Reflection: How does acknowledging your imperfections make you feel? What steps can you take to fully embrace them?

   _____

   _____

   _____

   _____

2. Can you think of a time when you had to find a creative solution to overcome a challenge?

   - Activity: Recall a specific instance where you used creativity to overcome a challenge. Write a short story about this experience.

   - Reflection: How has this experience influenced your approach to other challenges? What skills did you develop as a result?

   _____

   _____

   _____

   _____

3. Who do you turn to for support when facing challenges or insecurities?

- Activity: List the people you turn to for support and write about a time when sharing your struggles with them made a difference.

- Reflection: How has seeking support helped you navigate challenges?

- How has this changed your relationships and spurred personal growth?

_____

_____

_____

_____

4. How do you cultivate self-compassion and celebrate your uniqueness?

- Activity: Create a self-compassion toolkit and make a vision board that represents your uniqueness and individuality.

- Reflection: How do these practices make you feel about yourself? Which strategies work best for you and why?

_____

_____

_____

_____

## FIVE TIPS FOR SEEING YOUR TRUE COLORS

1. **Embrace Your Imperfections:** Reflect on your own unique challenges and acknowledge them as part of who you are. Understanding and accepting your imperfections is the first step toward embracing your true self.

2. **Be Creative in Overcoming Challenges:** Celebrate the creative solutions you find to navigate your challenges. Whether it's organizing your workspace in a way that suits you or finding alternative methods to complete tasks, your creativity is a powerful tool.

3. **Seek Support and Connection:** Recognize the importance of seeking support from others who may share similar experiences or offer empathy and understanding. Building a network of supportive people can help you navigate your challenges with confidence.

4. **Practice Self-Compassion:** Be kind to yourself, especially when dealing with feelings of embarrassment or insecurity. Practicing self-compassion allows you to move past negative emotions and focus on your strengths.

5. **Embrace Your Uniqueness and Authenticity:** Understand that your imperfections make you unique. Embrace them as part of your true self and live authentically. By doing so, you can fully appreciate your own journey and inspire others to do the same.

## SUMMARY

My journey with color blindness was transformative, teaching me invaluable lessons about acceptance and self-love. I now see it as a distinctive facet of my identity. Through creative problem-solving, unwavering support, and self-compassion, I found the courage to shed the burden of insecurity and embrace myself wholeheartedly.

This journey has shown me true beauty lies beyond physical appearances and societal standards. It's about understanding who you are and valuing your unique perspective. What imperfection will you choose to embrace today? Embrace your journey and let your true colors shine.

Seeing our true colors enables us to realize our deepest aspirations. It's about understanding who we are and what we truly want. In the next chapter, we'll delve into realizing these aspirations.

## CALL TO ACTION

I challenge you to reflect on your imperfections with kindness and understanding. Embrace them as integral parts of your unique identity, recognizing that true beauty transcends perceived limitations. What imperfection will you choose to embrace today? Which true colors are waiting for you to see? Embrace your journey, let your true colors shine, and unlock the potential within.

www.DerickSebastian.com

# CHAPTER 14

# REALIZING YOUR ASPIRATIONS

"You don't have to see the whole staircase, just take the first step."

— Martin Luther King, Jr.

**D**id you ever have a childhood dream that seemed out of reach only to find yourself unexpectedly closer to it years later? What happens when life redirects you, yet still leads you toward fulfilling your youthful aspirations in ways you never imagined? How do you respond when an opportunity suddenly arises, challenging you to step up and prove your readiness?

## MY STORY

Growing up, I always loved anything and everything about sports. I found excitement in competing and dreamt of becoming a professional athlete, specifically a Major League Baseball player. It didn't pan out the way I envisioned because my asthma got so bad in sixth grade. But that's when I found the ukulele, a humble instrument that introduced me to a whole new journey. However, I was always curious about how I could connect my musical journey to my childhood dream of becoming a professional athlete. This is how these two passions connected.

Back in 2007, I was having dinner at my in-laws. Raymi and I sat at the dining table watching the Lakers play a home game at Staples Center. It was a really good game, but what stuck out was seeing the Lakers logo at center court as the camera panned back and forth with each change of possession. I thought, Wow! I wonder how many basketball greats have run across the Lakers logo, especially when my favorites like Shaquille O'Neal and Kobe Bryant are playing.

I turned to Raymi and said, "I wonder what it would be like to play my ukulele at center court at Staples Center for the Lakers?"

She looked at me, paused, and stopped chewing her food. We gave each other blank stares for a few seconds, then laughed the idea away.

We saw the idea as a "yeah right" kind of thing—because let's face it, what ukulele player has ever played at Staples Center for the Lakers? The idea was too scary to even fathom, yet that night, the question kept knocking in my mind—"What if? What if my passion could become my profession?"

Everything happens for a reason, and only God's timing is perfect timing.

On a typical evening in 2010, I was performing one of my evening gigs at the Hula Grill in Kaanapali. A family of five sat at one of the front tables near the stage. They were so into the music they stayed the entire evening, waiting for me to finish my last set. They slowly slipped away as I was breaking down my equipment, but to my surprise, they came back the next evening and sat at the same table. I knew I had to meet them, so during the break before my final set, I went out to introduce myself.

We had an instant connection, as if we were already family. As we talked, the subject drifted to baseball. Are you kidding me? I love baseball. And to my jaw-dropping surprise, I found out I was talking with Derrick Hall, the CEO of the Arizona Diamondbacks, and his beautiful family. I was totally shocked. I couldn't believe it. Wow! Talk about God's timing.

Hall gave me his direct contact information and said, "If you're ever in Arizona, you need to give me a call."

Holy smokes! I had just met Derrick Hall. Talk about one of the coolest moments ever.

A few months later, I was booked for a summer West Coast tour with stops in Las Vegas and San Diego. I had a few days of downtime between cities and shows, so I thought maybe I should reach out to Mr. Hall to see if I could stop by Arizona to go to my first-ever MLB game. At twenty-nine, I had never attended an MLB game—professional baseball doesn't exist in Hawaii.

I called Mr. Hall, shared the details of my tour, and mentioned a possible detour to Arizona. He asked if I'd have my ukulele with me. I replied, "Absolutely. I'll have my full tour equipment with me."

Abruptly, Mr. Hall said, "Okay, let me call you back."

It felt strange, almost as if something urgent had come up. For the next thirty minutes, I couldn't stop wondering if I'd said something wrong. Then, my phone rang. It was Rob, the director of game operations for the Diamondbacks. He asked if I could play the national anthem on my ukulele. Without hesitation, I answered, "Yes, absolutely!"

"Great! Mr. Hall and the Arizona Diamondbacks would love to have you perform the national anthem at Chase Field," Rob said.

I accepted the invitation without a second thought.

We hung up, and I just sat there. I couldn't believe what had just happened. I was ecstatic. My body was jolting with pure joy and excitement.

But a big problem came to mind seconds later. I didn't know how to play the national anthem on the ukulele—I had never even tried. Holy smokes! What had I been thinking? What did I just do? It happened so fast—what had I got myself into? I was terrified because I had to learn the national anthem and be completely performance-ready in less than three weeks.

I wasted no time, spending hours researching different versions of the national anthem, from vocal to instrumental performances. I practiced, practiced, and practiced.

When the day finally came, it was surreal. Here I was at Chase Field, driving up to the VIP parking lot and entering through a back lobby. Trophies and awards were everywhere in shiny glass cases. A few Golden Glove awards, but even more cool, there it was—the 2001 World Series Trophy. It was so cool!

"Mr. Sebastian?" someone called my name.

It was one of the game operations assistants, who asked me to follow her. We went through a series of doors, down what felt like secret hallways, and finally through a long tunnel with a slight incline. Suddenly, there it was—the field. This tunnel was actually the players' tunnel leading to their dugout. I was awestruck. I could clearly hear the crack of the bat hitting balls—the "Whack" echoed through the stadium, and it was the coolest sound ever. I saw the players taking batting practice, talking, and casually getting ready before the game.

We walked onto the field through the Diamondbacks' dugout, and as I looked up, there was Mr. Derrick Hall holding a custom jersey with "SEBASTIAN" and the number twenty-one. It was incredible—twenty-one was the same number worn by one of my all-time favorite athletes, Deion Sanders.

I couldn't believe it. It truly felt like I had been drafted into the major leagues. I got to meet more of Mr. Hall's staff, took pictures, and even met Luis "Gonzo" Gonzalez, the World Series Champion from the 2001 D-backs. What a grand way to experience my first MLB stadium visit.

We eventually went through the game plan—all the details leading up to my performance. As I went through my sound check, I heard someone in the distance call out, "Howzit, Bruddah!" I immediately stopped and looked around because, hey, I was in Arizona at Chase Field, and this greeting was typically only heard back home in Hawaii.

A man walked up to me and introduced himself. "I'm Russ, VP of operations. I'm from Maui!"

Are you kidding me? I was even more shocked. Russ and I chatted for a while, talking about Maui and life. We had an instant connection. Boy, did I feel at home, and what a great way to be welcomed to Chase Field.

On June 9, 2010, I made history by being the first ukulele artist to perform the national anthem for the Arizona Diamondbacks at Chase Field. It was a reality check—my childhood dream come true. I may not have made it to the MLB as a player, but I had made it by playing my ukulele.

This achievement was undoubtedly one of the biggest highlights of my life, even though it wasn't for the Lakers at Staples Center…yet. It was an incredible milestone in realizing my aspirations. Then my mind started racing. What if? What if I could use this experience to perform in other stadiums and arenas, and ultimately, one day for the Lakers?

## WHAT I LEARNED

Timing is everything, and sometimes your plans for success take a detour, preparing you for something bigger and better than you imagined. Life has a way of redirecting you, not to frustrate you, but to position you for greater opportunities. Each twist and turn, each unexpected challenge, is a step in the journey toward your ultimate destination.

Manifesting your next vision requires more than just dreaming; it demands courage, determination, and a willingness to embrace unexpected opportunities. Dreams are the seeds of possibility, but action and perseverance are what make them flourish. It's about taking those dreams and transforming them into tangible goals, even when the path isn't clear.

My journey from aspiring athlete to ukulele performer at Chase Field epitomizes the power of dreaming big and seizing the moment. When my childhood dream of becoming a Major League Baseball player became unattainable due to asthma, I didn't abandon my passion. Instead, I found a new way to connect with my love for sports—through music. It wasn't the path I originally envisioned, but it was a path that led to a moment of triumph I could never have imagined.

Seizing the moment requires an open heart and a fearless spirit. It means being ready to say yes when opportunities arise, even if they seem daunting or outside of your comfort zone. When Derrick Hall offered me the chance to perform the national anthem at Chase Field, I didn't hesitate, even though I didn't yet know how to play the song on my ukulele. I trusted my ability to rise to the challenge and let my passion guide me.

The key to manifesting your vision is remaining adaptable and resilient. Life's detours often bring unexpected blessings and lessons essential for growth. Embrace each opportunity with gratitude and enthusiasm, knowing every experience is a valuable part of your journey.

In pursuing your dreams, remember success is not always about reaching the initial goal, but about the person you become along the way. Each step, each challenge, and each victory shapes you into a stronger, wiser, and more resilient person. By staying true to your vision and being open to where the journey takes you, you can achieve greatness beyond your wildest dreams. Through this journey, I also learned that with determination, it's possible to master a new song in less than three weeks—though I would recommend giving yourself more time.

**EXERCISE**

1.  Have you ever experienced an unexpected twist that turned out to be better than your original vision?

    - Activity: Write a narrative comparing your initial vision with the unexpected outcome, emphasizing the lessons learned from the unexpected turn of events.

    - Reflection: How did the unexpected outcome surpass your original vision? What does this teach you about being flexible and open to new opportunities?

    _____

    _____

    _____

    _____

    _____

    _____

    _____

    _____

2.  What seemingly impossible dream have you entertained, and how did it shape your journey?

    - Activity: Create a vision board that represents your impossible dream and the steps you've taken or plan to take to achieve it.

- Reflection: How has pursuing this dream influenced your personal growth and decisions? What can you do today to move closer to realizing this dream?

_____

_____

_____

_____

_____

_____

3. Reflecting on chance encounters, what unexpected connections have significantly changed your journey?

- Activity: List three chance encounters that had a significant influence on your life and describe how each connection changed your path.

- Reflection: What do these encounters teach you about the importance of networking and being open to new relationships?

_____

_____

_____

_____

4. Have you ever hesitated when presented with an opportunity? How did you overcome your doubts and take action?

- Activity: Think of a time when you hesitated about taking an opportunity and write about the factors behind your hesitation and how you eventually took action.

- Reflection: What strategies helped you overcome your doubts? How can you use those strategies for future opportunities?

_____

_____

_____

_____

_____

_____

_____

_____

_____

_____

_____

_____

_____

_____

**FIVE TIPS FOR REALIZING YOUR ASPIRATIONS**

1. **Believe in the Impossible:** Despite the odds, dare to dream beyond conventional boundaries. By daring to entertain big ideas, you open yourself up to unforeseen possibilities and remarkable opportunities.

2. **Embrace Unexpected Connections:** Every encounter holds the potential to change the course of your life. Be open to meeting new people and forming connections because they can lead to extraordinary opportunities you never could have imagined.

3. **Seize Every Opportunity:** When opportunity knocks, be ready to answer. Even if you feel unprepared or hesitant, take the chance. Embrace the moment because it could set in motion significant events in your journey.

4. **Prepare for Success:** Success often requires relentless preparation and unwavering dedication. Invest time and effort into mastering your craft, ensuring you are ready when your moment arrives. Your dedication will pay off when the opportunity presents itself.

5. **Embrace Unexpected Twists:** Life rarely follows a linear path, and sometimes detours lead to greater destinations. Recognize that your journey might not unfold as you envisioned, but it can exceed your expectations in unexpected ways. Embrace these twists as part of your unique path to realizing your aspirations.

## SUMMARY

My journey from aspiring athlete to ukulele performer shows the power of daring to dream big and embracing unexpected opportunities. Believing in the impossible laid the groundwork for remarkable achievements. Chance encounters underscore the importance of remaining open to serendipitous connections. Seizing opportunities requires both readiness and courage, highlighting the significance of overcoming doubt and fear. Diligent preparation is paramount. While my initial dream did not materialize, the experience at Chase Field surpassed my expectations, emphasizing the importance of embracing unexpected twists and turns on the path to success.

Several key lessons emerged. First, the power of dreaming beyond conventional boundaries cannot be underestimated. Second, know that adaptability and openness to new connections can lead to life-changing opportunities. Third, readiness to seize opportunities as they arise, even when you feel unprepared, is crucial. Fourth, thorough preparation and relentless dedication are essential for success. Finally, embracing unexpected twists can lead to destinations even greater than your original dream.

Realizing aspirations is a significant step, but achieving them often requires persistence and politeness. These qualities can open doors and create lasting impressions. Next, let's explore how perfecting these traits can lead to success.

## CALL TO ACTION

As you pursue your own vision, I challenge you to dream bigger than you ever thought possible, to dare to dream beyond convention, and to embrace the unexpected opportunities that come your way. Seize each moment with unwavering courage and determination. Reflect on your aspirations—what bold vision are you manifesting? How will you harness the power of preparation, adaptability, and relentless dedication to turn your dreams into reality? Consider how you can apply the lessons learned from my journey to your own pursuit of greatness. Embrace these principles and embark on your path with confidence, knowing the twists and turns along the way may lead you to destinations even greater than you imagined.

www.DerickSebastian.com

# CHAPTER 15

# PERFECTING YOUR PERSISTENT POLITENESS

"As long as we are persistent in our pursuit of our deepest destiny, we will continue to grow. We cannot choose the day or time when we will fully bloom. It happens in its own time."

— Denis Waitley

Have you ever had a dream that seemed out of reach, one you couldn't shake, even when it felt impossible? To what lengths would you go to make that dream a reality? How do you stay motivated when faced with numerous setbacks and no guarantees of success? What does it take to keep pursuing a goal, year after year, when the outcome is uncertain?

**MY STORY**

In 2011, I took another huge leap as I embarked on my first-ever international ukulele tour in Australia. It was a monumental moment because one of my biggest dreams as an artist was to travel internationally and share the gift of ukulele. It finally happened. And as a bonus, to my surprise and honor, I was also invited back for an encore performance of "The Star-Spangled Banner" for the Arizona Diamondbacks at Chase Field.

Things just kept getting better and better. I felt some kind of momentum with this "national anthem on the ukulele" concept. I became a unique ukulele artist breaking into the major sporting events scene and finally making a splash internationally. I mean, how cool is that? Already two performances at Chase Field and now an international ukulele artist? Super cool.

But to my dismay, in 2013, Mr. Ellis passed away. It was an extremely difficult time. I felt he had become my angel of endless opportunities because the floodgates had opened up for me.

Shortly after Mr. Ellis's passing, from 2013 to 2016, my life became a whirlwind. I did a TEDx Talk in Santa Cruz, California, and I had more amazing opportunities to expand worldwide, doing international ukulele tours in Thailand, the Philippines, South Korea, China, Canada, Germany, Finland, and Estonia. It was non-stop craziness. I was on the road at least one hundred days a year during that time. I had incredible momentum moving forward.

Even though things were happening and I felt like I was on top of the world, one question constantly nagged at me: "How in the world can I play at Staples Center for the Lakers and be on ESPN's *SportsCenter*?"

It was a crazy idea planted in my mind in 2007. In 2010, I finally found the courage to reach out to the Lakers, shortly after my first national anthem performance for the Arizona Diamondbacks.

I cold-called the Lakers, scared out of my mind. While attempting my first call, my hand was shaking so badly. I would dial the number but, just before dialing the last few digits, hang up. I rehearsed out loud what I planned to say, talking it through over and over, driving myself insane.

Finally, I made my first call to the Lakers, hoping to speak to someone directly, but I was directed to a voicemail. I left a message after the beep: "Aloha. I'm Derick Sebastian, and I'm an ukulele artist from Maui. I'm calling to inquire about the possibility of performing the national anthem on ukulele for the LA Lakers at Staples Center." I left my number and email, hoping for a quick response. A few days went by—no call back. After a few weeks—still crickets. Just nothing.

I called the Lakers again and, surprisingly, they gave me a direct email address to the game operations department. I didn't get a name, but it was a lead, at least. I emailed the Lakers directly, but again, no reply for several weeks.

After about a month of trying to get a hold of the Lakers without luck, I decided to take another route. I called the Lakers again and asked for their fax number (yes, fax number; I am that old), which I easily got this time. I guess the Lakers operator was familiar with my voice by then. I put together a professional presentation with a cover letter and my artist profile and faxed it to the number. The status was "successful," so I knew someone received my fax at the Lakers office.

But still, crickets. No response at all—no email replies, no call backs, not even a fax reply. Nothing. Zero. Absolute silence.

I consistently tried reaching out for nearly six months but got no reply. It was really deflating, and I was somewhat discouraged because I tried so much and nothing happened. It felt like a waste of time, and I had to ask myself, "What am I chasing here? Is it worth it? Is it something that would fulfill my journey? Why do I desire this big stage?"

One quiet afternoon, I sat down and felt a cool breeze—and all the answers flowed within me. "Yes, it is worth it. I'm chasing my dream, and it gets me excited. It fuels me because I'm being me, accepting I'm different, courageous, and brave enough to step outside of my comfort zone and simply try." This realization got me up every morning and allowed me to daydream with a purpose, a calling to inspire and seek out my life's journey.

I made a conscious and consistent effort to reach out to the LA Lakers every offseason, trying to plant a seed of opportunity. I did so for five straight years, not being aggressive but simply practicing polite persistence.

Sure, it was discouraging at times, but I never gave up. Something told me one day, at the right time, it would happen. I had to be strong; I had to manifest the opportunity in my mind and think positively moving forward.

Then one typical afternoon, after years of making calls, leaving voicemails, sending numerous emails, and even faxing updates to the Lakers, I found myself in the midst of my daily routine—picking up my kids from school and shuttling them to their afterschool activities and baseball practices. It was a bit hectic, and we were running late, but the boys were hungry, so I decided to make a quick stop at McDonald's. As we were pulling out of the drive-thru, my phone rang. It was a 310 area code, which I immediately recognized as being Los Angeles. But, being on "daddy duty," there was no time to answer.

After all the drop-offs, I finally had time to check my voicemails, and one of them was from the 310 number. I played it and couldn't believe what I heard—I was totally shocked! It was the famous ex-Laker Girl, Lisa Estrada, who was the director of game operations at the time.

She asked if I was interested in performing the national anthem on ukulele for the Lakers' preseason opener at Oahu's Stan Sheriff Center. Wow! Are you kidding me? Absolutely!

I called Lisa back that same afternoon, my heart racing with nerves. She answered immediately, and we spoke, connected well, and confirmed the details. Although it was a tight squeeze in my schedule, I managed to fit this Lakers opportunity on Oahu in between my US West Coast tour and Asia tour. It wasn't the Staples Center in LA, but it was the Lakers, and I thought if I could prove myself at the preseason game, it might eventually land me in LA for the real deal.

On October 4, 2015, it happened. I was standing center court at Oahu's Stan Sheriff Center, performing the national anthem for the LA Lakers and Utah Jazz. It was a huge success, especially being right at home in Hawaii. Most importantly, the Lakers were happy with the result.

After the Lakers experience on Oahu, I came home to Maui for a few days before heading off for a two-week tour in South Korea. I was still on a high from the Lakers performance while I was on tour in South Korea. It had made the news throughout the islands, and my anthem performance went viral on several social media platforms.

I couldn't believe it. Connecting with and playing for the Lakers was a huge success, but for some reason, it felt sort of incomplete because it wasn't at Staples Center.

I spent a long two weeks touring in Asia right around the holidays, and when I got home, I finally had some time to rest, recuperate, and reflect. Before long, I started getting phone calls to travel to LA, kicking off the new year with more music meetings and opportunities.

Then an exciting, yet crazy-scary idea struck me. While in LA, what if I piggybacked all these upcoming music meetings and private events and made a run at performing at Staples Center for the LA Lakers?

I emailed Lisa from the Lakers, telling her I was coming to LA and wanted to see if there was any possibility of playing the national anthem on ukulele at Staples Center for the Lakers.

She emailed me back within minutes, and our conversation went on for nearly half an hour. We were going back and forth so fast I didn't even realize my long-time dream was about to come true.

But it was confirmed. After nine years of manifesting this crazy idea, on March 10, 2016, I made history by becoming the first-ever ukulele artist to perform the national anthem for the LA Lakers at Staples Center! It was also a milestone game, a complete sellout with 20,000 fans witnessing the last time Kobe Bryant and LeBron James played against each other before Bryant's retirement.

That very same night, after the game, my national anthem performance was featured on a thirty-second clip on ESPN's *SportsCenter*. My vision had become my passion, which had become my profession. Right then and there, I realized daydreaming with purpose actually works.

The evening's accomplishment was featured all over the news in Hawaii and the LA area, and my videos went viral all over social media.

It was a dream come true—an experience I'll never forget. This journey taught me the value of mastering polite persistence and never giving up on your dreams.

## WHAT I LEARNED

Never give up on your dream because your dream will never give up on you! This journey has shown me that persistence and determination are key ingredients in turning dreams into reality.

I learned that polite persistence is not just about repeatedly asking for what you want; it's about doing so with respect, humility, and unwavering belief in your vision. It's about understanding timing is everything, and sometimes the Universe is aligning things in the background while you continue to push forward.

Embracing the journey is just as important as reaching the destination. Each step, each small victory, and even each setback taught me invaluable lessons. They strengthened my resolve and sharpened my focus. I realized the obstacles in my path were not meant to stop me but to prepare me for the greatness that awaited.

I also discovered the power of connections and serendipitous encounters. Meeting Derrick Hall and eventually performing at Chase Field, and then receiving that call from Lisa Estrada, were moments that seemed to come out of nowhere. Yet they were the result of continuous effort and being open to opportunities wherever they may arise.

Ultimately, this journey taught me the importance of having faith in the process. Dreams may take time to materialize, and the road may be long and winding, but persistence, patience, and positive thinking can make even the wildest dreams come true.

So, no matter how daunting the path may seem, keep moving forward. Trust in your journey, believe in your dream, and never underestimate the power of perfecting your persistent politeness.

Never give up on your dream because your dream will never give up on you! This journey has taught me that persistence and determination are the keys to turning dreams into reality. Every "no" wasn't rejection, but redirection, bringing me closer to my goal.

Polite persistence isn't just about asking repeatedly; it's about doing so with respect, humility, and belief in your vision. Timing is everything, and sometimes the Universe is working behind the scenes as you keep pushing forward.

I've learned that embracing the journey is just as vital as reaching the destination. Every victory and setback taught me invaluable lessons, preparing me for the greatness ahead.

Unexpected connections—like meeting Derrick Hall and Lisa Estrada—didn't happen by accident. They came from continuous effort and staying open to opportunity.

In the end, this journey taught me to have faith in the process. Dreams may take time, but with persistence, patience, and belief, even the wildest dreams can come true. Keep moving forward, trust your journey, and never underestimate the power of polite persistence.

**EXERCISE**

1. Have you ever had to be persistent in achieving your goals?

   - Activity: Write a narrative about a time you had to persist to achieve a goal, detailing the challenges, strategies used, and outcome.

   - Reflection: How did this experience shape your understanding of persistence and its importance in your future goals?

   _____

   _____

   _____

   _____

   _____

   _____

   _____

   _____

   _____

2. How do you balance persistence with respect when pursuing your goals?

   - Activity: Create a list of guidelines to ensure your persistence remains respectful and considerate.

- Reflection: How can maintaining politeness and respect enhance your ability to achieve your goals?

_____

_____

_____

_____

_____

_____

3. How do you adapt your strategy when faced with setbacks?

- Activity: Write about a recent setback and how you adapted your approach to overcome it.

- Reflection: What did you learn from adapting to this challenge, and how can these lessons be applied to future obstacles?

_____

_____

_____

_____

_____

_____

_____

_____

4. How do you maintain patience and resilience while pursuing long-term goals?

- Activity: Develop an action plan with techniques for maintaining patience and resilience, like meditation or setting short-term goals.

- Reflection: How do these practices help you stay motivated and focused on your long-term objectives?

_____

_____

_____

_____

_____

_____

_____

_____

**FIVE TIPS FOR PERFECTING YOUR PERSISTENT POLITENESS**

1. **Consistent Outreach:** Consistent and respectful communication is key. Whether you're following up on emails, making polite phone calls, or sending courteous reminders, maintain a steady presence while respecting boundaries. Your persistence can make a significant difference. Additionally, by consistently reaching out, you build and strengthen your network.

2.  **Adaptability:** Be willing to adapt your approach if necessary. If your initial attempts don't yield results, try different methods like sending a fax instead of an email or reaching out through another channel. Flexibility allows you to navigate obstacles and find alternative paths to success.

3.  **Patience and Resilience:** Persistence requires patience and resilience. Even when facing periods of silence or setbacks, remain resilient and continue your efforts. Remember that progress often takes time, and setbacks are just part of the journey.

4.  **Maintain Positivity:** Stay positive and optimistic, even in the face of rejection or silence. Positive energy can be infectious and may open doors that were closed before. Keep believing in yourself and your dreams, and let your positivity shine through.

5.  **Celebrate Small Wins:** Acknowledge and celebrate each small victory along the way. Whether it's a positive response to an email or a step forward in the process, recognizing these milestones keeps you motivated and energized for the journey ahead.

## SUMMARY

If you really believe it, you will achieve it. If you daydream with passion, your visions will be realized. Persistence coupled with politeness and resilience is a powerful tool for achieving your goals. Remember, if you truly believe in your goal and persistently pursue it with grace and determination, success is within reach. Consider how you can integrate the principles of polite persistence into your approach. Think about how you can adapt your strategies when faced with obstacles and remain flexible in your methods. Recognize the value of patience and resilience in your journey. And celebrate the small wins along the way; they are important milestones that keep you motivated and energized.

Politeness and persistence pave the way, but true success comes from embodying greatness every day. It's about consistently striving to be your best self. Next, let's see how daily greatness shapes our journey.

## CALL TO ACTION

I challenge you to reflect on a goal you've been pursuing and consider how you can apply the principles of polite persistence to enhance your approach. What steps can you take to maintain consistent effort while respecting boundaries and remaining resilient in the face of obstacles? Embrace your journey with faith, knowing each step brings you closer to mastering polite persistence and achieving your dreams. This is the essence of perfecting your persistent politeness.

www.DerickSebastian.com

# CHAPTER 16

# CONNECTING WITHIN YOUR SIX DEGREES OF SEPARATION

*"Ask for help. Not because you are weak, but
because you want to remain strong."*

— Les Brown

The year 2023 was everything I had dreamed of—it was all about baseball. No, not playing the sport, but performing the National Anthem at Major League Baseball stadiums around the country. It all started in March with a whirlwind five-stadium tour during Spring Training in Arizona, where I connected and performed at Camelback Ranch, Peoria Sports Complex, Salt River Fields at Talking Stick, Sloan Park, and Tempe Diablo Stadium. It was non-stop craziness, but a history-making experience I'll never forget.

The Spring Training tour went so well that I was invited to expand the tour and perform during the regular season for the San Francisco Giants, Seattle Mariners, and Los Angeles Dodgers. I was beyond excited—this was the very thing I had manifested for years. "What if I could do a regular season National Anthem tour for Major League Baseball?" And now it was happening. But as with any great achievement, there were challenges along the way—ones I never expected.

Before the big West Coast tour, the logistics alone were enough to stress anyone out. Every team had its own unique way of handling things, and working through those details was no easy task. But that was just the beginning. A few days before my first performance for the Giants, I was in my hotel room, going through my pre-show checklist—in-ear monitors, cables, pedals, battery packs—it all looked good. But then I went to check the battery pack on my ukulele's pickup system. What should have been a simple routine check turned into a nightmare.

As I tried to change the battery, the connector started to split apart—a malfunction that had never happened before. I didn't think too much of it at first, but something didn't feel right. Later that evening, I went to do a sound check on my ukulele at a friend's performance spot, and that's when it all went downhill. My ukulele started making an explosive, popping sound—like fireworks going off every time I strummed. No matter what I did, I couldn't fix it. Panic set in.

It was late Thursday night, and my performance for the Giants was just thirty-six hours away. My backup ukulele was 2,500 miles away in Maui. I called every resource I had back in Maui and in the Bay Area—no one had a performance-grade ukulele I could borrow. I even reached out to friends who were airline pilots, hoping they could help fly my backup in, but no luck. I was stuck.

In desperation, I went live on social media, explaining the situation to my followers, hoping for a miracle. My phone blew up with calls, texts, and messages. People offered advice, but the best option seemed to be overnight shipping my backup ukulele from Maui to San Francisco—with no guarantee it would arrive in time.

I paced outside the closed restaurant, overwhelmed by disbelief. "What am I going to do? Should I cancel the Giants' performance? I can't go on stage with a malfunctioning ukulele and let everyone down." It was one of the most stressful moments of my life. Late that night, I went back to my hotel, numb, feeling like everything I had worked so hard for was slipping away. I broke down in tears because I was in complete disbelief. But I knew something had to work out.

I was sitting on the couch in complete silence when suddenly my phone rang. A dear friend, a pilot from Maui, had seen my video and heard my voicemail. "Derick, I can help," he said. "I've got a plan, but you need to trust me. Have your wife drop off your ukulele to me right now. Tomorrow morning, I'll run it up to the gates and pass it off to my friend, another pilot, who's flying the Maui to San Francisco route. He'll be landing at SFO in the early evening, and he'll meet you in the lobby of the airport hotel. I promise you, your ukulele will be hand-delivered to you tomorrow evening. Just trust me on this because you're playing the national anthem for the Giants on Saturday."

Not even thirty minutes later, I received another call—this time from a friend of a friend, a professional touring guitar tech who worked at Allegro

Music, a local shop across the bay. He offered to fix my ukulele's pickup system first thing Friday morning.

I was overwhelmed with gratitude and relief—I cried tears of joy!

Since it was now the wee hours of Friday morning, I tried to get some sleep, but it only lasted four hours. My mind was already on a mission, and I had no time to waste. I woke up, drove from Burlingame across the San Mateo Bridge to Fremont, immediately got my ukulele's pickup system repaired, then rushed north to Oakland for a production meeting. After that, I rushed back across the bay to San Carlos for another meeting, and as some of you may know, the traffic on the 880 Freeway on a Friday is no joke! But I survived, and I made it! The time finally came—I headed up to the Grand Hyatt at SFO to meet my friend's pilot friend.

I anxiously paced back and forth in the hotel lobby, thinking, "Is this really happening? What if my ukulele didn't make it? This is absolute craziness!" Minutes later, my phone pinged with a message: "Our crew is on the train and just one stop away." *Really?* I thought.

I was so nervous. I couldn't believe it was all coming together. Then, the elevator doors opened, and here comes a flight crew walking out, laughing, and having a good time. And what did I see? A pilot walking right up to me, carrying my custom, metallic, navy blue Calton Case, and inside it— my brand-new, backup custom Kanilea Ukulele!

I vaguely remember, but my guess is I hugged him about five times! A few of those hugs probably squeezed the air right out of him. I was beyond words—ecstatic, in pure joy and gratitude.

Talk about adrenaline. In less than twenty-four hours, I had both my repaired ukulele and my backup in hand—just in time for the Giants' game.

On June 24, 2023, I performed the National Anthem for the Arizona Diamondbacks and San Francisco Giants at Oracle Park. A week later, on June 30, I performed at T-Mobile Park for the Tampa Bay Rays and Seattle Mariners. Finally, on July 5, I closed out the tour at Dodger Stadium, performing for the Pittsburgh Pirates and Los Angeles Dodgers.

Each performance was historic, making me the first ukulele artist to ever perform the National Anthem at these iconic stadiums. But more than that, the anticipation, the challenges—from the panic to the overwhelming stress—taught me that even when things seem impossible, there's always a way.

It's that tiny mustard seed of hope and trust that somehow, someway, everything will work out because God is always good, and the Universe has your back. This is the heart of *Connecting Within Your Six Degrees of Separation*—knowing that help is always closer than you think, and that through faith, trust, and openness, the right people and solutions will appear when you need them most.

## WHAT I LEARNED

This experience taught me that sometimes, no matter how much you plan and prepare, life throws unexpected challenges your way. It reminded me that having faith, trust, and the humility to ask for help are as essential as hard work. No matter how impossible the situation may seem, solutions are often already in motion—you just have to be open to receiving them.

I learned that relying on others is not a sign of weakness but a powerful strength. Help is always closer than we think, but we must allow ourselves the space to ask for it and believe that it will come. This journey reinforced the importance of staying calm, trusting the process, and knowing that God and the Universe have a way of aligning things when you need them most.

When we trust in the people around us, when we have faith in something bigger than ourselves, and when we stay open to unexpected help, we find that challenges often lead to unexpected blessings.

**EXERCISE**

1.  Trusting the Process

    •   Question: How comfortable are you with trusting the process when things feel out of your control?

    •   Activity: Reflect on a recent challenge where you felt out of control. Write down the steps you took to navigate the situation, and identify where trust, either in yourself or others, played a role. If you didn't lean on trust, think about how the outcome might have been different if you had.

    •   Reflection: How can trusting the process and the people around you change your perspective in future challenges?

    _____

    _____

_____

_____

_____

_____

2.  Reaching Out for Help

    • Question: Are you comfortable asking for help when you face
      obstacles?

    • Activity: Think about a situation in your life where you felt stuck.
      List the people or resources you could have turned to for help. Now,
      reflect on a current challenge and make a list of potential people
      who might support you in finding a solution.

    • Reflection: What's one small step you can take today to reach out
      for help in an area where you need support?

_____

_____

_____

_____

_____

3.  Recognizing Connections

    •   Question: Have you ever considered how your connections could play a role in overcoming obstacles?

    •   Activity: Write down the names of people in your life who have helped you in unexpected ways. Consider the networks, friendships, and relationships you've built. Now think about how you can strengthen these connections moving forward.

    •   Reflection: How do these connections demonstrate the importance of being open to receiving help?

    _____

    _____

    _____

    _____

    _____

    _____

4.  Visualizing Faith in Action

    •   Question: How do faith and trust play a role in your ability to stay calm during stressful situations?

    •   Activity: Close your eyes and visualize a moment when you were overwhelmed, but something unexpectedly worked out in your favor. Write down how you felt during the process and how it turned around for you.

- Reflection: How can you apply this faith and trust in future moments of stress or uncertainty? What daily practices can help you strengthen your belief in the power of connection and trust?

_____

_____

_____

_____

_____

_____

## FIVE TIPS FOR CONNECTING WITHIN YOUR SIX DEGREES OF SEPARATION

1. **Ask for Help Early:** Don't wait until things become unmanageable before reaching out for support. Asking for help isn't a sign of weakness—it's a strength. Recognize when you need help and reach out early to people in your network who can guide or assist you.

2. **Nurture Your Relationships:** Your connections can open doors to opportunities, but they must be nurtured. Stay in touch, offer help when you can, and build genuine relationships based on trust and respect. You never know when these connections will come full circle and play a vital role in your journey.

3.  **Be Open to Unexpected Solutions:** Help can come from the most un-expected places. Stay open-minded and be willing to receive support in ways you might not have anticipated. The solution may already be in motion, but it's up to you to be open to seeing it.

4.  **Trust the Process:** When challenges arise, it's easy to feel overwhelmed. Trust there's a process unfolding, even if you can't see it right away. Have faith that the right people and circumstances will align at the right time if you continue to move forward.

5.  **Stay Calm in the Storm:** During moments of stress and uncertainty, it's crucial to stay calm and grounded. Panic can cloud your judgment, making it harder to see the help that's available. Take a deep breath, trust in your connections, and know that solutions are within reach.

## SUMMARY

In life, challenges will come your way no matter how much you plan and prepare. What I've learned through my experience is that help is always closer than you think—often just a connection away. By having faith, trusting the process, and allowing yourself to ask for and accept help, you open the door to solutions you may not have seen coming.

This chapter emphasizes the importance of nurturing relationships, staying open to unexpected support, and remaining calm in times of uncertainty. When you trust God, the Universe, and the people around you, even the toughest situations can become opportunities for growth. Your connec-tions—whether through family, friends, or unexpected sources—are there to help you succeed. Embrace Connecting Within Your Six Degrees of Separation, and you'll find you're never alone on your journey.

**CALL TO ACTION**

I challenge you to embrace Connecting Within Your Six Degrees of Separation. Take a moment to reflect on the people in your life and how they can help you overcome obstacles, support your dreams, and guide you on your journey. Don't be afraid to ask for help when you need it, and trust that the Universe will align the right people and resources at the right time. Take that step, reach out, and allow others to walk alongside you as you pursue your purpose. Your success is closer than you think—tap into the power of connection, faith, and trust.

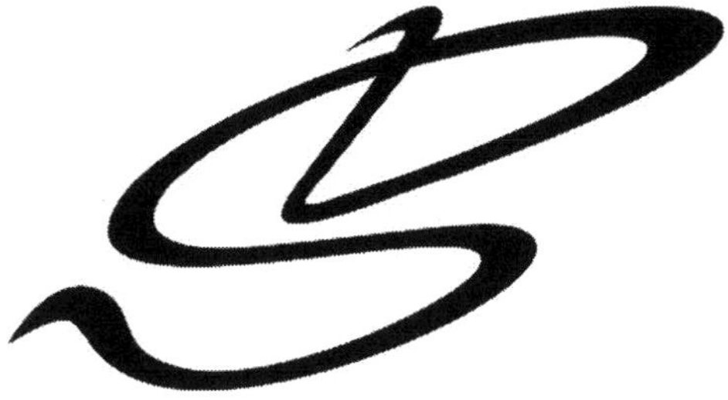

# SECTION 5:

# THRIVING IN YOUR TRUE PATH

"The meaning of life is to find your gift. The
purpose of life is to give it away."

— Pablo Picasso

# DOWNLOAD AND STREAM SONG FOR FREE!

www.DerickSebastian.com/DearMe

# DEAR ME

## Song Written and Performed by Derick Sebastian

I don't wanna see you cry no more

Don't worry about the things you can't control

You're not alone


And people will throw their stones at you

Don't ever throw it back

Keep it to build a better path


It doesn't matter how much you fall

It matters when you stand 'cause you can call


Dear me

Don't listen to the noise

Every day is a choice, to hear my voice

Dear me

Don't ever second-guess

Of your success

'Cause life's a beautiful mess

When you feel like giving up, don't fear

Your breakthrough is near

Keep the faith 'cause I am here


The light is shining down on you

Keep doing what you do

'Cause life is from a bird's eye view

www.DerickSebastian.com

www.DerickSebastian.com

# CHAPTER 17

# FLOWING WITH YOUR LIFE'S CURRENTS

"Be water, my friend. Empty your mind, be formless, shapeless—like water. Now you put water in a cup, it becomes the cup. You put water into a bottle it becomes the bottle. You put it in a teapot it becomes the teapot. Now water can flow, or it can crash. Be water, my friend."

— Bruce Lee

How do you navigate life's unexpected storms? When the world turns upside down and everything you planned is suddenly out of reach, how do you find the strength to keep going? Have you ever faced a moment when you had to adapt quickly to a new reality, unsure of what the future would hold? How do you cope with the weight of uncertainty and the effects of events beyond your control? As you reflect on these questions, consider how you can flow with life's currents, finding resilience and hope even in the midst of chaos.

## MY STORY

As 2019 was coming to an end, I was gearing up for what promised to be the busiest year of my music career. I had a full schedule of performances lined up, including corporate events, private functions, major sporting events, and the beginning of my journey as a wedding officiant, which opened up even more opportunities in the wedding industry. Heading into 2020, I was booked solid for the entire year—it was absolutely crazy. Life was good.

But then you all know what happened in March of 2020—the lockdown quickly took over and forced the world to come to a complete stop. On March 11, 2020, I was performing for a private event in beautiful Kapalua, Maui. The event sponsors had booked the entire Ritz-Carlton, but my show that night was only for the top 100 representatives—before the wave of 1,500 more company representatives flew in the next day.

It was a high-end gig, and the energy was awesome; we were all having a good time. I came back on stage after a quick break and some company announcements, ready to close the night with another forty-five minutes of playing time. As I was just getting into my last set, I was abruptly asked to take another break. The president of the company took the microphone to make another announcement, but this time, the tone of his voice was concerning, as if he were panicking.

He composed himself, but his voice was still shaky when he said something like, "Aloha, ladies and gentlemen. This is surely a night to celebrate your success, but we have some concerning world news. This virus is rapidly spreading across the world, and the President closed off the United States border just a few minutes ago. I hate to do this, but I need to cancel this event now and send everyone home to be close to your families. I will have the 1,500 representatives who were supposed to come in tomorrow turned around and sent back home as well. I don't want anyone to be stuck; I just want you all to be home with your families. Please rest assured, all accommodations will be taken care of by our management and events team, who will be working around the clock to make this happen. We are ending tonight's event immediately so we can all make the journey back home first thing tomorrow morning. Take care and be safe."

Wow! I was speechless. I looked around, and everyone had a blank stare on their faces—the room had fallen completely silent. It was unnerving. The company reps, guests, hotel staff, and vendors were dumbfounded. I could feel the anxiety and panic developing in the room, but everyone composed themselves as they slowly got up and left the ballroom. And there I was, all alone with the hotel staff, wondering what the heck had just happened.

I overheard bits of conversation along the lines of how something really bad was about to happen. "Whatever it is, we're all going to be affected." I'd never experienced anything like this. In my entire music career, I'd never had an event cancel in seconds with everyone being sent home. I can't even describe exactly how it felt.

I took a few deep breaths, said some prayers, and started slowly breaking down my equipment.

It was a long drive home. I called Raymi to tell her what had happened, and that was it. I drove home in complete silence, knowing deep down inside that the lockdown was about to change the world.

Within two weeks of that night, every booking filling my schedule in 2020 was canceled.

The world stopped, and we all lived in complete stillness. No one was working except from home, our kids were home doing virtual learning, no visitors were coming to Maui, the beaches were empty and wide open, stores were closed, and no one was outside. If you did see anyone, like all of us, they were wearing masks because they were scared of whatever this was. It was eerie.

My wife, boys, and I made the best of our time. We went to the beach at least three times a week, swimming, bodyboarding, and cliff diving. We hung out, cooked, ate, and yes, we all gained weight, including our little dog, Ziggy. We drove around Maui, exploring places we never had time to see before. Raymi had a well-deserved break from work; I concentrated on songwriting and producing music while the boys focused on finding their creative sides, including drawing, photography, and videography.

Despite the uncertainty and forced time off from playing shows, we made the best of our time together. We surely connected and enjoyed each other's company until the lockdown ended and life returned to normal.

Three-and-a-half years later, everything changed on Maui again. The afternoon of August 8, 2023, I was in Wailuku picking up our youngest, Jackson, from football practice. It was a beautiful, normal, but slightly windy afternoon. We didn't yet know something was happening on the opposite side of Maui—people were experiencing hell.

While Raymi and I were waiting for practice to end, she frantically showed me a few social media posts saying Lahaina was on fire. I couldn't believe what I was seeing. That evening, I tried calling my friends and family in the Lahaina area, but no one answered. I soon learned there was no electricity or phone service there. Even more shocking, I learned certain places had no water . A few hours later, we learned the Upcountry and Kihei areas were on fire too.

It felt like Maui was on fire. Part of me died that night because deep down inside, I knew people were not just losing their homes or workplaces; people were suffering; so many were dying. It was one of the saddest and most helpless days of my life. I wanted to help, but the area was closed off. Knowing you were either outside the fire area looking in for a way to help, or inside wishing to get out was unbearable.

Every social media feed I saw, including YouTube, was filled with horrific videos of the fires all around Maui, but mostly Lahaina. Everything was on fire. People were screaming, crying, panicking, yelling, and running. Many were even in the ocean to try to get away from the fires. Every news outlet around the world was talking about our Maui fires. We were devastated. I couldn't believe what was happening.

A few weeks after the fire, I learned all my close friends, whom I consider family, were accounted for, though some of their loved ones were not. I felt a deep need to connect with Lahaina in my own way. Fortunately, I was able to drive over to the Lahaina area to try to process what my mind couldn't fully grasp.

My heart broke, and I cried the entire time as I made my way into West Maui. I simply couldn't believe what I was seeing—it was beyond devastating. Everything was burnt to the ground: homes, cars, buildings. Blackened ruins were everywhere. The streets were a mess, littered with garbage, and telephone and electric poles lay scattered. Lahaina looked like it had been bombed.

The strong, scorched, strange smell is something I'll never forget. When the wind shifted, I could even smell the aftermath of the fires over the West Maui Mountains, fifteen miles away as a bird flies.

I kept driving and driving. I didn't even realize I was already in Kapalua, which is about ten minutes past Lahaina. I ended up sitting on the beach for a long time just feeling my feelings and praying. I knew this fire was life-changing for our community and possibly the world.

Lahaina is and always has been close to my heart. The people and the place give me hope because it's where my music career actually started—performing in West Maui. Some of the venues were gone, and even more heart-wrenching, some of the people I worked with lost their lives and most were displaced. No home, no job, no money, and for some, no family.

After some weeks, I couldn't process the Maui fires. My mind was completely overloaded, so I consciously decided not to watch the news and to stay off social media.

Raymi and I ended up helping at the local shelters around Maui. Although I knew I was doing good deeds, I wasn't prepared for the experience. I simply could not process what I was seeing. So many people were packed into the gym that I couldn't even see the floor. People were everywhere, sleeping, crying, lying on makeshift beds, some even bandaged from burns. Some just had blank, uncomprehending faces. It was like a Third World country. Once I found some courage to talk to the fire victims, their stories sank my heart. As they talked, it was as if I was living out the very moments that happened to them. It was deep, dark, and heavy, but I kept talking to individuals and families because I knew it was what they needed.

What I didn't realize was that I'm only human, so I can only take in so much. I eventually became depressed in a dark space and had to seek help and counseling from close friends and my local church.

A month after the fires, Maui felt like it had shut down again. It was like a second global lockdown. No one was coming to Maui; it became quiet, still, and deserted. The people of Maui again lost jobs or got laid off, and small businesses took another major hit.

The ripple effect hurt our Maui community in so many ways. Even today, people are still mourning and we have more questions than answers. But through all this, I learned to accept the flow of life, understanding that despite the chaos and heartbreak, a path forward always exists. This acceptance, along with the unwavering support of my family and community, helped me navigate these dark times, reminding me how important it is to adapt and find strength even in the most challenging circumstances. That is the essence of flowing with life's currents. Everyone on the island was hurt economically, even if they didn't live near the fires. And we all had to move on and rebuild together. Our mantra became: *Maui Strong*!

**WHAT I LEARNED**

The Maui fires changed my life, my thinking, and my perspective. Experiencing such profound loss and devastation made it painfully clear that nothing is permanent or guaranteed. Tomorrows aren't promised to anyone. Taking life for granted is a luxury none of us can afford.

I realized I can't control everything, but I can control how I respond. I can choose to let heartbreaking experiences harden my heart, or I can choose to let them open my eyes to the preciousness of every moment. The latter is the path I chose, and it has made all the difference.

Love became the cornerstone of my daily life. It's easy to get caught up in the busyness and stress of our routines, but in the face of tragedy, the love we share with one another is what helps us move forward. Love is what binds us, heals us, and gives us the strength to take the next step, even when the way ahead is shrouded in uncertainty.

I learned to cherish the simple joys of life: the laughter of my children, the comforting presence of my wife, the beauty of a sunset, and the serenity of a quiet beach. These moments, though small, are the threads that weave the fabric of a fulfilling life. They remind me of what truly matters and keep me grounded in the midst of chaos.

The Maui fires also taught me the importance of community. The outpouring of support and solidarity from friends, neighbors, and even strangers was overwhelming. It reinforced the idea that we are not alone in our struggles. We are all connected, and our collective resilience helps us rebuild and recover.

Embracing this perspective has brought me a deeper sense of purpose. I am more committed than ever to using my music and my platform to spread love, hope, and positivity. I want to be a beacon of light for others, just as so many have been for me during these challenging times.

Every day is an opportunity to make a difference, no matter how small. Whether it's through a kind word, a helping hand, or a heartfelt song, we all have the power to be a positive influence for those around us. These acts of love and kindness are where we find true meaning and fulfillment.

The lesson of impermanence and the power of love have reshaped my approach to life. I strive to live each day with intention, gratitude, and a heart full of compassion. By doing so, I honor the experiences that shaped me and ensure I am always moving forward, guided by the light of love and resilience.

**EXERCISE**

1.  How do you accept and adapt to life's unexpected changes?

    • Activity: Reflect on a recent unexpected event. Write about your initial reaction and how you adapted. Consider what helped you accept the change and what you learned from the experience.

    • Reflection: How did this change realign your perspective on life? What did you learn about your capacity to adapt and be more resilient?

    _____

    _____

    _____

    _____

2.  Who supports you during uncertain times, and how can you strengthen these relationships?

    • Activity: List your key emotional and practical support people. Reflect on ways to nurture these relationships, such as regular check-ins or offering support in return.

- Reflection: How do these relationships enhance your resilience? What actions can you take to deepen these connections?

_____

_____

_____

_____

3. Which activities give you a sense of purpose, and how can you incorporate more of them into your routine?

- Activity: Identify activities that bring you joy and fulfillment. Make a plan to incorporate at least one of these activities into your daily or weekly routine.

- Reflection: How do these activities enhance your overall well-being? How can you ensure you make time for them regularly?

_____

_____

_____

_____

4. How can you contribute positively to your community during a crisis?

- Activity: Brainstorm ways to support your community during times of need. Choose one action, such as volunteering or organizing an event, and make a plan to implement it.

• Reflection: How does contributing to your community make you feel? What do you hope to achieve, and how can you measure your progress?

_____

_____

_____

_____

## FIVE TIPS FOR FLOWING WITH YOUR LIFE'S CURRENTS

1. **Embrace Change and Uncertainty:** Life is inherently unpredictable. Accepting this fact allows you to respond more flexibly and resiliently to changes. Embrace the unexpected. See it as an opportunity for growth and adaptation.

2. **Find Strength in Relationships:** Quality time with loved ones can bring immense support and happiness, especially during uncertain times. Strengthen your relationships by being present, offering support, and appreciating the people who matter most to you.

3. **Pursue Meaningful Activities:** Engaging in activities that bring you joy and a sense of purpose can provide stability and fulfillment. Whether it's a creative hobby, volunteering, or learning something new, find something that resonates with you and make it part of your routine.

4. **Contribute to Your Community:** Helping others can bring a profound sense of purpose and fulfillment. Look for ways to support your community, whether through volunteering, donating, or simply offering a helping hand to those in need. Your actions can make a significant difference.

5. **Practice Gratitude and Resilience:** Cultivate a habit of gratitude for what you have and develop resilience in the face of challenges. Reflect on the positive aspects of your life, appreciate the small moments, and stay strong through adversity. These practices can help you navigate life's ups and downs with a positive mindset.

## SUMMARY

In this chapter, I talked about how the unexpected disruptions of 2020 and the devastating Maui fires reshaped my understanding of life's unpredictability and the importance of adapting. These events taught me to appreciate the present, embrace the support of loved ones, and engage in activities that not only bring joy but also serve a greater purpose. By accepting the flow of life with an open heart and a resilient spirit, I've learned to navigate the twists and turns with grace and gratitude, always ready to contribute positively to those around me. I realized life is a series of unpredictable events that can either break us or shape us into stronger, more compassionate people. Embracing change rather than resisting it allows us to find new opportunities for growth and fulfillment. Loved ones' support becomes a cornerstone during these times, providing the emotional strength we need to persevere. Engaging in meaningful activities not only brings joy but also helps anchor us during turbulent times.

Flowing with life means accepting all parts of our journey, including regrets. Embracing regrets allows us to learn and grow from them. Next, let's delve into how to embrace and learn from our regrets.

## CALL TO ACTION

I challenge you to reflect on a time when life took an unexpected turn. How did you handle it? What can you do now to better accept and flow with change? Consider how embracing life's unpredictability can enhance your resilience and overall happiness. By flowing with your life's currents, you can navigate the ups and downs with grace and find peace in the journey, knowing each twist and turn is an integral part of your personal growth and fulfillment.

www.DerickSebastian.com

# CHAPTER 18

# EMBRACING YOUR REGRETS

"We do not remember days; we remember moments."

— Cesare Pavese

W hat have you let slip away because of doubt or hesitation? Have you ever regretted missing an opportunity that was right in front of you? How often do you take for granted the time you have with the people who matter the most? What steps can you take today to ensure you don't miss out on the precious moments and opportunities that come your way?

**MY STORY**

Back in 1996, I entered the first annual Maui Player's Ukulele Contest at the Hula Grill, located on the beautiful beachfront of Kaanapali. It was a two-day event: the first day was preliminaries, and the second day was the finals.

I was only in eighth grade, and boy, was I nervous because it was the first "real" contest I had ever entered.

I only had a few months to prepare, so I practiced around the clock. I wanted my performance to be perfect, and ultimately, I wanted to make it to the finals.

The day of the contest was a gorgeous Saturday morning. I made the drive with Mr. Ellis from Kahului, passing along the breathtaking Pali coastline. Although I was extremely nervous, I had a really good feeling about this contest.

At the Hula Grill, I was surprised to find it was like a big concert. So many contestants were checking in and already practicing on their ukuleles. A breakfast buffet was laid out for everyone, and a lot of parents and visitors were trying to get tables. Servers and staff were moving around quickly. The stage was decked out with a huge sound system. Local celebrity musicians were there as contest judges. Radio disc jockeys were present as MCs. Everyone was taking pictures with everyone else. Vendors were selling their arts and crafts. People were setting up lawn chairs on the outside grass area, and curious onlookers were slowing down to see what was going on.

One of the coolest parts was several ukulele icons were holding workshops and jam sessions for anyone with an ukulele who wanted to join. It was huge! I could feel the energy and excitement; it was like the main event on West Maui. It was the place to be.

When the ukulele contest was about thirty minutes from starting, the event staff gathered us contestants together in our respective age divisions. It was an embracing welcome, and after briefing us on the contest rules, they went over the judging sheet: ten points for attire, ten points for introduction, ten points for mannerism, ten points for ukulele accuracy, ten points for technique, ten points for complexity, ten points for singing, ten points for originality, ten points for stage presence, and ten points for overall performance.

*Wait, what? Ten points for singing?* I thought. *Wait a minute, I don't sing. I didn't prepare a song to sing. This is an ukulele contest, not a talent competition. Why are they judging us on singing?* I completely freaked out inside. *Oh, my goodness, what am I going to do?*

I was extremely lucky to have Mr. Ellis there by my side, supporting me in my first ukulele contest.

After the briefing, I ran to Mr. Ellis and frantically told him about the contest judging us on singing.

"I don't sing, and I didn't prepare to sing a song. What should I do?"

He took a deep breath and chuckled.

I panicked and asked, "Why are you laughing? I'm freaking out here!"

"Relax, my boy," Mr. Ellis calmly told me. "Everything happens for a reason. If you don't get any points for singing, then so be it. Your job is to perform your best with what you prepared to perform. At the end of the day, you're not here to win the contest; you're here to share your God-given gift of music with everyone here and do it sincerely from your heart. If you do that this weekend, no matter what the outcome, you've already won."

I appreciated his great wisdom and advice so much. Talk about perspective.

It took me a while to get it all together, but I did. I made it through the preliminaries and went on to the following day, placing second in the finals. And yes, the judges later told me, "It was because you didn't sing. However, if you had sung, you would have easily won your division."

Honestly, I remember being very happy with my performance. I was content and knew I had done my best. Many people came up to me offering praise, but still, there was that little competitive part of me that said, "I wanted to win. I hate losing."

Shortly after the contest, as we were packing up and getting ready to leave, I heard a voice call out, "Mr. Derick Sebastian." I stopped and looked—it was Eddie Bush, one of my ukulele heroes, who was serving as one of the judges.

This man was considered one of Hawaii's greatest ukulele virtuosos. Eddie Bush performed at nearly every major venue in Waikiki, including the Canoe House at the Ilikai, the Tapa Room at the Hawaiian Village, and the Hawaii Visitors Bureau show in Japan. He also appeared on *The Tonight Show* with Johnny Carson, *The Mike Douglas Show*, and on Merv Griffin, Ed Sullivan, Lawrence Welk, and Johnny Cash's shows. He was even honored by the Hawaii State Legislature because of all his accomplishments.

I couldn't believe it. Eddie Bush had gone out of his way to find me? It was surreal.

He said, "Derick, I absolutely love your playing style. You did an amazing job. I'd love to keep in touch and help you throughout your ukulele journey."

I couldn't believe this ukulele great took the time to praise me and offer his support.

Honestly, although on paper I placed second in the contest, that moment confirmed that I still won within myself and beyond the contest. By doing my best and simply intending to share my ukulele gift with people, a miracle had happened—because meeting and connecting with Eddie Bush was surely a miracle.

Eddie and I became very close friends. I visited and spent time with him at his home on Oahu. We talked about life, music, and dreams. At every Hula Grill Ukulele Players Contest, we got together before the event and talked about my ukulele arrangements for the contest. He was extremely supportive and sincerely wanted the best for me.

We started to connect so well Eddie said he wanted to take me outside of Hawaii, perhaps on a tour in the US and even possibly internationally.

Wow! That was some huge news to process. To be honest, I was scared of imagining that. It freaked me out because I felt I wasn't good enough. You know—that good old voice in your head called "imposter syndrome."

Every time Eddie brought up touring, I put it off by saying, "Yeah, okay. Let me think about it."

Eventually, after years of putting off all of Eddie's ideas and opportunities for me, the unimaginable happened.

On September 10, 2002, Eddie Bush died of a massive heart attack. He was gone just like that. I was shocked. I couldn't believe it. I just sat in my car, completely still, knowing I had missed out on a lot. I had passed on Eddie's generosity because I was simply thinking about myself and how scared I was.

I deeply regretted not making the best of my time with Eddie while he was here. He had big dreams for me, but my dreams weren't big enough. I was too into myself, and ultimately, I took him for granted, thinking all his travel and touring plans would eventually happen for us.

I felt so bad. I had missed opportunities. Eddie was a friend who was not only looking out for me but trying to give me a chance to expand and experience the world.

After all, I hadn't taken the opportunities. I missed the Eddie Bush train.

A few years after Eddie's passing, I finally got a grip on myself and got it all together. It was difficult to overcome the regret I had, but I slowly gained the perspective and courage to emote through my music. From this internal emotional experience, I ended up writing an instrumental composition in honor of Eddie, called "Eddie Bush Tribute."

At first, I was hesitant to perform the song because the story behind it carried so much regret, but something told me to keep performing the composition, so I did. I always told the story of how this amazing man could have picked any other ukulele player to work with, but he chose me. He poured his love and knowledge into me, even giving me multiple chances to travel the world with him, but I just wasn't ready. I felt like I had let him down.

My instrumental, "Eddie Bush Tribute," has now taken me all over the world because various stages and events have requested I perform the song.

Looking back, I realize it doesn't matter what happened to me; what matters is what I do about it. Although I may not have made the best of my time with Eddie, I now know not to take anything for granted, especially life itself. This is the essence of owning your regrets.

In hindsight, that initial experience at the Hula Grill Ukulele Contest was a pivotal moment. When I realized I had lost because I didn't sing, I could have let it defeat me. Instead, I was motivated to improve and challenge myself. I began taking voice lessons from the amazing Joy Fields, a vocal coach who helped me find my voice. Through her guidance, I became comfortable enough to sing and play simultaneously, blending my voice with my ukulele. This newfound confidence led me to win the Hula Grill Ukulele Contest four consecutive years after that. Now, I genuinely enjoy singing and playing, and I've explored the world expressing myself through my voice. It is a testament to the power of persistence, learning, and growth—principles Eddie Bush always encouraged in me.

## WHAT I LEARNED

I can never take anything for granted, especially the love that surrounds me. Because one day, it'll be gone.

This realization hit me hard. The experience with Eddie Bush was a turning point, teaching me that opportunities and the people we cherish are fleeting. It's so easy to get caught up in the busyness of life, assuming there will always be more time, more chances, more moments to connect. But life has a way of reminding us that nothing is guaranteed.

Eddie's sudden passing showed me the importance of being present and fully appreciating the people in my life. Every moment spent with loved ones is a gift. We need to show our appreciation and gratitude openly and often. We need to embrace every opportunity to express our love and make memories that will last a lifetime.

This lesson isn't just about personal relationships. It's also about seizing every opportunity that comes our way. Whether it's a chance to travel, to learn something new, to perform on a new stage, or to meet someone who could change our lives, we need to grab these moments with both hands. We can't afford to be passive or assume these chances will come again.

Living with this awareness has made my actions more intentional. I strive to be fully present, to listen more, and to engage more deeply with those around me. I've learned to prioritize what truly matters, letting go of trivial worries and focusing on what brings genuine joy and fulfillment.

Eddie's legacy lives on through the lessons he taught me. His encouragement and belief in my potential pushed me to overcome my fears and doubts. By embracing the opportunities he offered, even posthumously, through my tribute song, I was able to honor his memory and share his influence with the world.

The essence of owning your regrets is not dwelling on missed opportunities but using those experiences to grow and change for the better. It's about understanding every moment is precious and we should live with intention, gratitude, and an open heart.

**EXERCISE**

1.  Which regret often weighs on your heart, pulling you away from the present?

    -   Activity: Reflect on a specific regret that frequently influences your thoughts and emotions. Write a letter to yourself describing the regret, how it makes you feel, and why it affects you so deeply.

    -   Reflection: How does this regret influence your daily life and interactions? What steps can you take to bring yourself back to the present moment when this regret arises?

    _____

    _____

    _____

    _____

2.  Which regret have you been avoiding, and what's the first step toward facing it?

    -   Activity: Identify a regret you've been avoiding. Write down why you've been avoiding it and the emotions associated with it. Then, outline the first step you can take to acknowledge and address this regret.

    -   Reflection: How might facing this regret help you grow and move forward? What support or resources might you need to take this first step?

_____

_____

_____

_____

3.  What lesson did you learn from a regret that could guide your future decisions?

    -   Activity: Choose a regret and write a short essay about the lesson you learned from it. Reflect on how this lesson has influenced your behavior and decision making.

    -   Reflection: How can you apply this lesson to future decisions? What practical steps can you take to ensure you don't repeat the same mistake?

    _____

    _____

    _____

    _____

4.  How can sharing your own story of regret help others learn from your experiences?

    -   Activity: Write a story about one of your regrets and how you've grown from it. Share this story with a close friend, family member, or through a blog or social media.

- Reflection: How did sharing your story make you feel? How can your experiences help others who might be dealing with similar regrets?

_____

_____

_____

_____

## FIVE TIPS FOR EMBRACING YOUR REGRETS

1. **Recognize and Accept Your Regrets:** Acknowledge the opportunities you missed due to fear or self-doubt. Recognizing your regrets is the first step toward learning from them and moving forward.

2. **Learn from Past Mistakes:** Instead of dwelling on what went wrong, focus on the lessons these experiences teach you. Use your reflections to seize moments more courageously in the future.

3. **Share Your Experiences:** Turn your regrets into messages that resonate with others by sharing your stories. This not only honors the people or moments you regret but also helps others learn from your experiences.

4. **Transform Regret into Action:** Use the energy of regret to motivate positive change and action. Channel your feelings into activities that honor the effects of those regrets and lead to growth and fulfillment.

5.  **Forgive Yourself and Move Forward:** Self-forgiveness is crucial for moving past regrets and keeping them from defining you. Accept that you did your best with the knowledge and emotions you had at the time, and use that understanding to move forward with a positive mindset.

## SUMMARY

This chapter was about the poignant lesson of a missed opportunity with my mentor Eddie Bush, whose sudden passing left me with deep regrets about unseized moments. This experience underscored how important it is to cherish life and seize opportunities when they arise. By accepting and owning these regrets, I learned valuable lessons about taking initiative, embracing courage, and the importance of acting on life's opportunities. This chapter highlights how owning your regrets can lead to personal growth and a renewed commitment to living fully.

I realized regrets are a natural part of the human journey. They serve as powerful reminders of our vulnerabilities and the finite nature of life. Instead of allowing regret to paralyze you, use it as a springboard for action and self-improvement. Moreover, sharing your regrets can lead to healing that connects you with others who have experienced similar feelings. Through this collective understanding, we can find strength and encouragement to face future challenges with resilience.

Embracing regrets is a step toward harnessing the power of Aloha. This spirit of love, peace, and compassion can transform our lives. Next let's see how embracing Aloha has shaped my path.

## CALL TO ACTION

I challenge you to reflect on a regret that significantly changed you. How can you use this regret as a catalyst for personal growth? What steps can you take to ensure you seize opportunities more boldly in the future? By embracing your regrets, you can transform them into powerful motivators that guide you toward a more fulfilling and courageous life.

www.DerickSebastian.com

# CHAPTER 19

# HARNESSING YOUR POWER OF ALOHA

"A person who has the Spirit of Aloha loves
even when the love is not returned."

— Rev. Abraham K. Akaka

What does Aloha mean to you? How do you embody the Spirit of Aloha in your daily life, and how does it shape your interactions with others? Have you ever stopped to appreciate the simple moments and connections that bring Aloha into your life? As you think about your own journey, ask yourself: How can I harness the power of Aloha to create a deeper sense of purpose and fulfillment in everything I do?

**MY STORY**

When I first started playing the ukulele in the sixth grade, my sole focus was on mastering the instrument. I was obsessed, constantly asking myself, "How can I get better at the ukulele every day and ultimately master this four-string instrument?" Maybe I was a little too obsessed, but I'd like to think it was a good thing—it kept this young eleven-year-old kid's mind occupied and gave me something meaningful to do.

After about a year of playing, I felt like I was really gaining momentum. I believed I could play anything! My progress was quick, and the one person who truly noticed was Mr. Ellis.

Mr. Ellis and I had our daily get-togethers during school, but I began to notice something changing. It wasn't just about jamming on the ukulele anymore; our time together became more conversational. He'd ask me about my dreams, what excited me, and what challenges I was facing. He'd even ask about my fears and what was bothering me. We talked about life.

Mr. Ellis wasn't just a school security guard or a mentor—he became my best friend.

One thing he always emphasized was the importance of building great relationships. At the time, I didn't fully understand what he meant. One day, after school, while sitting on a bench, I finally asked him, "How do I create great relationships by playing the ukulele? Isn't it just about focusing on my talent and skills?"

Mr. Ellis smiled, took a deep breath, and paused.

He said, "My boy, I want you to fully understand this with all your heart: Anyone can sit in their room and learn how to be a good ukulele player— that's what I call being a musician. But if you learn to not only play the ukulele but also give back, share your talent, tell the stories from your heart, and connect with people through your gift—that's what I call being an entertainer. And *that*, my boy, is what makes you a great ukulele player."

"Entertainer?" I asked.

"Yes," Mr. Ellis replied. *"If you want to be great, your mission is to move people emotionally and inspire them through your ukulele. You need to entertain them, take them away from their everyday struggles, make them smile, make them laugh, and remind them that they are loved."*

From that moment, Mr. Ellis and I became partners in crime. We played at school assemblies, for teachers in their classrooms and staff meetings, at random basketball courts, and at every family gathering. I swear, Mr. Ellis took me to every single one of his aunties and uncles' houses, and we played for them too!

We played for any and every opportunity that came our way, and boy, did we have fun!

It was through these experiences that I finally understood: the ukulele wasn't just an instrument—it was a tool to connect with people and build relationships. It was through the smiles, the laughter, and the shared stories of life's ups and downs that we truly became *ohana* (family).

And that's when I realized the true meaning of living Aloha.

There's something special about being born and raised here in Hawaii. There's a certain magic in the air, a sense of ease that comes with each breath. The sun, fresh air, blue sky, ocean waves crashing, birds chirping, and the everyday trade winds all contribute to this feeling. The sunrise and sunset, the neighboring islands, the people, even strangers, all share a smile of love. The energy in Hawaii is like nowhere else on earth—everyone here is happy!

For me, it's easy to take this for granted because I was born and raised here on Maui. But it became clear to me when I started traveling the world, especially when leaving Raymi and our boys behind. My appreciation for family, love, and relationships has deepened. I used to worry about what others thought, how I looked, or even just being myself. Now all that matters is being surrounded by amazing family and friends, having good food on the table, fulfilling my life's purpose, and inspiring others. I have no room for drama or disputes. I strive for honesty and humility, living *pono*—being righteous and doing what is right.

This is Aloha, and Aloha is *everything*.

Aloha is love, loving everyone. Aloha is a state of mind. It's about trying your very best not to judge but to see the good in every person. It's the smile you give, the handshake and hug. Aloha is making sincere eye contact and asking, "How are you doing?" It's being there for one another, sharing life's stories—the ups and downs and everything in between. Aloha is sharing happiness and joy, failures and successes. Aloha is home—the inviting spirit, loving unconditionally. It's about never giving up on yourself or others, knowing you have a gift, a calling, and a purpose. Aloha is God, your Lord and Savior.

Aloha is a way of life, an attitude. It's about relationships and how you make people feel. It's finding your true self in acceptance, not taking anything for granted, and being grateful for what you already have. Aloha is appreciation and respect, being humble. It's embracing what life has to offer and truly being in the moment. Aloha is you. Aloha is me. It's all of us! It's wherever your two feet are standing, being present right here, right now. Aloha is breathing in and out, deeply to your core. It's being grateful despite your circumstances, being at peace not just with others, but within yourself.

Aloha is accepting who you are, not what you do. It's being authentic to yourself and to the world. It's laughter and being the love and light to others' souls. Aloha is winning at life no matter what, and being in a pure state of joy, not just happiness. It's inspiration, being open to your callings and signs in life. Aloha is family, and family is everything. It's about leaving no one behind, loving strangers, and sending out good vibes and thoughts to whoever comes to mind.

Aloha is to forgive, to pray. It is God, the universal intelligence. It's a spirit that everyone has; Aloha is love. Aloha is being okay even when you're not okay. It's allowing yourself to be yourself. Aloha is being in the moment and winning your given day and opportunity. It's caring and realizing life is bigger than who you really are.

Aloha is contagious and can never be stopped. It's life; it's healing, a sense of calmness and peace. It's good energy, good vibes. Aloha is operating on a high frequency, bringing out the best in each other, being encouraging, being love and light. Aloha is helping each other walk home. It's being present, sharing the breath of life. Aloha is you and me. It's being compassionate and confident in what you have to offer the world, sharing, caring, and giving.

Aloha is heartfelt, being understanding, pausing, and being still. It's listening first and talking last. Aloha is taking one day at a time, being brave and courageous even when you're scared and uncertain. It's taking risks, knowing there is no such thing as failure—only life's lessons learned. Aloha is not where you're at; it's who you are becoming. It's unconditional love, guidance, and a compromise. It's co-existing with one another and helping each other walk home.

Aloha is patience, not just with everyone around you, but within yourself. It's not about being right, but doing right. It's being fluid, knowing everything happens for a reason. Aloha is truly having grace and believing life doesn't happen to you; it happens for you. It's a journey, a purpose, a calling, a way of life. Aloha is silence and being at peace. It's winning at life; it's me and you.

Aloha is more than just a word; it's a profound philosophy, a lifestyle, a way of being, of loving, that shapes our daily lives and interactions. It is the essence of what makes Hawaii a unique and beautiful place, not just in its physical landscape but in the hearts and spirits of its people. Living with Aloha means embracing each moment with gratitude and a deep sense of connection to everything around us. It means recognizing the beauty in the simple things, from the rustle of the palm leaves in the breeze to the warmth of the sun on our skin. It means understanding we are all part of something greater than ourselves, and our actions, no matter how small, can have a positive influence on the world.

Aloha is also about resilience and strength. It's about facing challenges with a positive attitude and an open heart. It's about knowing that no matter what life throws at us, we have the inner strength to overcome it. It's about being kind to ourselves, giving ourselves grace during tough times, and trusting everything will work out as it should.

Embracing Aloha is embracing life in all its forms, with all its ups and downs. It's about finding joy in the journey and peace in the present moment. It's about giving and receiving love freely and openly. Aloha is the guiding light that helps us navigate life's complexities, reminding us to stay true to ourselves and treat others with kindness and respect.

Aloha is the essence of this place called Hawaii. It's about harnessing the power of Aloha. My goal with my music, my ukulele, my voice, and my songs is to share the Aloha Spirit with everyone around the world. I hope to achieve this and make it my lasting legacy.

## WHAT I LEARNED

Aloha is the true power of love and light. It's more than just a word—it's a way of being that transforms lives through kindness, compassion, and connection. Living with Aloha means embracing unconditional love and seeing the good in every person and situation, just as Mr. Ellis taught me. He showed me that true greatness isn't just about mastering a skill, but about building relationships, sharing your heart, and connecting with others through your gifts.

Aloha is about giving and receiving, fostering deep connections and a sense of community. Mr. Ellis believed that the ukulele wasn't just an instrument but a tool to create those connections and spread joy. It taught me that my purpose wasn't just to play music, but to move people emotionally and lift them up, embodying the Spirit of Aloha.

Aloha also represents resilience and strength, giving us the courage to face challenges with an open heart. Mr. Ellis emphasized the importance of navigating life with love and compassion, creating a ripple effect of positivity wherever we go.

This is the essence of Aloha: using your gifts not just for yourself, but to inspire and uplift others, creating meaningful relationships and spreading light, just as Mr. Ellis helped me understand.

**EXERCISE**

1.  Describe the Aloha Spirit that lives within you.

    *   Activity: Reflect on the qualities embodying your unique Aloha Spirit. Write down at least three characteristics, such as kindness, compassion, or patience.

    *   Reflection: How do these characteristics show up in your daily life? What steps can you take to cultivate and strengthen them?

    _____

    _____

    _____

    _____

    _____

    _____

    _____

    _____

    _____

    _____

2. How can you incorporate acts of kindness into your interactions with others?

- Activity: Make a list of simple acts of kindness you can perform daily, like smiling at a stranger or offering a helping hand. Practice at least one act of kindness each day for a week.

- Reflection: How do these acts of kindness affect you and those around you? What have you learned from this practice?

_____

_____

_____

_____

_____

_____

_____

_____

_____

3. How can you deepen your connections with those around you and foster a sense of community?

- Activity: Organize an activity that brings people together, such as a community dinner or group hike. Focus on creating meaningful connections and fostering a sense of belonging.

- Reflection: How did this activity change your relationships and sense of community? What did you learn about the importance of connection and togetherness?

_____

_____

_____

_____

_____

4. How can you cultivate a spirit of gratitude and humility in your daily life?

- Activity: Start a gratitude journal and write down three things you are grateful for each day. Reflect on these entries at the end of the week and observe how they've changed your perspective.

- Reflection: How has focusing on gratitude and humility changed your outlook? What benefits have you noticed in your interactions and overall well-being?

_____

_____

_____

_____

_____

## FIVE TIPS FOR HARNESSING YOUR POWER OF ALOHA

1. **Cultivate Love and Acceptance:** Embrace the essence of Aloha by loving everyone and striving not to judge but to see the good in every person. Focus on fostering an environment of acceptance and understanding in your interactions.

2. **Express Kindness and Compassion:** Practice Aloha through simple gestures like offering a smile, handshake, or hug. These small acts of kindness can brighten someone's day and create a ripple effect of positivity.

3. **Build Meaningful Connections:** Be present for one another, sharing life's stories, joys, and challenges. Invest time in building and nurturing relationships that bring fulfillment and support to your life.

4. **Live with Gratitude and Humility:** Embrace gratitude for what you have and approach life with humility. Recognize your blessings and appreciate others' contributions, fostering a sense of contentment and appreciation.

5. **Be a Source of Light and Inspiration:** Share your Aloha spirit with others by being a beacon of positivity, encouragement, and support. Let your actions and words inspire those around you, creating a community of warmth and kindness.

## SUMMARY

The essence of Aloha transcends mere words; it's a feeling, a way of being that permeates every aspect of life in Hawaii. Born and raised on Maui, I've come to understand Aloha isn't just a greeting or a concept—it's a profound philosophy that shapes interactions, relationships, and the very fabric of existence. Aloha is about cultivating love, acceptance, and kindness toward oneself and others, building meaningful connections, expressing gratitude, and living with humility. Aloha encourages us to be sources of light and inspiration, spreading positivity and encouragement wherever we go.

But Aloha isn't something you can teach—it's something you must embrace with an open heart and mind. Once you do, it becomes part of who you are, guiding your actions and shaping your perspective on life. It's your responsibility to share the gift of Aloha with the world, enriching the lives of those around you and fostering a more compassionate and fulfilling existence for all.

The power of Aloha is instrumental in manifesting our dreams. It's about channeling positive energy and intentions toward our goals. Next, let's explore how to turn dreams into reality.

## CALL TO ACTION

I challenge you: How can you incorporate the principles of Aloha into your daily life? How can you embody love, compassion, and humility in your interactions with others? Embrace and harness the power of your Aloha

Spirit, and let it transform not only your life but the lives of those around you. I encourage you to join me in spreading the Spirit of Aloha throughout the world.

I invite you to sprinkle the Aloha spirit everywhere you go, every day of your life. When you do, you will manifest your passions into your profession.

www.DerickSebastian.com

# CHAPTER 20

# MANIFESTING YOUR DREAMS

"If you believe, you can do anything!
But you need to make up your mind."

— Sam Ellis III

I'm a daydreamer, a deep thinker. I'm not afraid to venture into those uncomfortable thoughts and ask myself, "What if?" What if I could do that? What if I could meet that person? What if I just said "yes" and saw what happened? What if I simply took a chance? What if you took a chance on manifesting your dreams? What if you daydreamed with purpose?

## MY STORY

When I first started playing the ukulele in 1993, as a sixth grader, I was completely captivated. Without YouTube or social media, I turned to TV for inspiration, and nothing excited me more than watching the Na Hoku

Hanohano Awards—the Grammys of Hawaii. I was in awe of the top local artists, dressed in tuxedos, being celebrated for their music, and I dreamed of one day being in that spotlight, even though it felt impossible. But in 2010, that dream became reality when my first ukulele instrumental album, From His Heart, was nominated for a Na Hoku Hanohano Award. I wore a tux, walked the red carpet with my wife, who was seven months pregnant with our son Jackson, and experienced the thrill of hearing my name called for Ukulele Instrumental Album of the Year. Though I didn't win, being there was a huge accomplishment and a dream come true.

Growing up, one of my all-time favorite music artists was Jason Mraz. I loved not only his music style but also his songwriting. After attending several of his concerts, I fell in love with his work and asked myself, "What if I could meet Jason Mraz and perform with him on stage?" I didn't just stop at asking; I visualized it, felt the excitement, and took steps toward it. Manifestation accomplished—I got to meet Jason and perform with him. It was amazing! Standing on stage next to someone who had inspired me so deeply was surreal. It felt like a dream, yet it was my reality because I dared to dream it.

I've always loved sports—competition is in my blood. If I could watch one TV channel for the rest of my life, it would be ESPN. I dreamed of becoming a professional athlete, maybe in baseball or football. I asked myself, "What if I could play the ukulele on a Major League Baseball field?" I visualized the crowd, the energy, and the honor of playing the national anthem. Manifestation accomplished—I performed the National Anthem for the Arizona Diamondbacks and Atlanta Braves at Chase Field in Phoenix, Arizona. The roar of the crowd, the feeling of standing on that vast field, it was everything I had imagined and more.

Then the question became, "What if I could make it to the NBA and play my ukulele at center court at Staples Center for the LA Lakers? What if I could get featured on ESPN's *SportsCenter*?" In just one night, manifestation accomplished—I made history as the first ukulele artist to play for an LA Lakers home game at Staples Center. And there I was on national television, featured on a thirty-second clip on ESPN's *SportsCenter* with Neil Everett and Stan Verrett. Standing center court, with the spotlight on me, playing my heart out, was a moment of pure triumph and gratitude.

Next, I wondered, "What if I could perform the national anthem more and become the first ukulele artist to do a national anthem tour?" I performed at Staples Center two more times, an encore for the Lakers and another for the LA Clippers. I did multiple national anthem tours for MLB, performing at various stadiums including Chase Field, Peoria Sports Complex, Salt River Field, Sloan Park, Oracle Park, T-Mobile Park, and Dodger Stadium. Each performance was a testament to the power of dreaming big and taking bold steps toward those dreams.

I also asked myself, "What if I could one day be a TEDx speaker?" Manifestation accomplished—I spoke about my father figure and mentor, the late Sam Ellis III, at TEDx. Standing on that red dot, sharing my story, and honoring Mr. Ellis, was a profound and humbling experience. It was a full-circle moment, connecting my past, present, and future.

"What if I could travel the world, touring, performing, and teaching the ukulele?" Manifestation accomplished—I've toured the United States, Australia, Thailand, the Philippines, South Korea (five times), China (twice), Canada, Germany, Finland, and Estonia. Each country brought new experiences, new audiences, and new opportunities to share my passion for music. Traveling the world with my ukulele felt like living a dream every single day.

"What if I could find a residence on Maui at a well-established resort and start an ukulele program?" Manifestation accomplished—I became a cultural practitioner at the Andaz Maui at Wailea, teaching ukulele and performing in the hotel's lobby and lounges. Sharing my love for the ukulele with visitors from all over the world right in the heart of my home island was a dream come true.

I love animation, especially Disney's Pixar films. I asked myself, "What if I could connect and perform for Pixar Animation Studios?" Manifestation accomplished—I held private ukulele workshops, performed for their animation department, and at several movie premieres. Walking through the halls of Pixar, seeing the creative energy and enthusiasm, was incredibly inspiring. It felt like my dreams were woven into the magic of storytelling.

"What if I could get my songs on the local radio?" Manifestation accomplished—I now have songs in rotation on local radio stations. Hearing my music on the airwaves, knowing it was reaching people, was a moment of deep satisfaction and joy.

"What if I could diversify in the local wedding industry and become a wedding officiant?" Manifestation accomplished—I'm now a busy wedding musician and officiant. Being part of such a significant moment in people's lives, sharing their joy and love, is incredibly rewarding. It's another way my music and passion have found a meaningful outlet.

"What if I could become a songwriter and producer and tap into the world of music licensing?" Manifestation accomplished—I'm now a songwriter, composer, and producer, with songs signed to established music libraries such as Warner Chappell PM, Sky Urbano, and Atrium Music, and I have composed for Roxy Quicksilver and Hyatt Worldwide. Each composition, each project, is a new adventure and a new opportunity to create something beautiful and meaningful.

"What if I could write a book and become a bestselling author and a professional speaker?" This book is guiding me on that path, bringing me closer to turning this dream into a reality.

"What if I could have an amazing wife and celebrate fifty years of marriage? What if I could be the father of three boys and eventually be a grandfather?" I'm blessed with a wonderful marriage, three incredible sons, and the journey of fatherhood is leading me toward the joy of being a grandfather one day. Each moment with my family is a cherished part of this unfolding dream.

Dreams do come true, and it all starts with manifesting them. The key to manifesting your dreams is to imagine you've already accomplished them. See yourself making it happen and being successful. See it, feel it, and embrace it. When you get excited about your thoughts or dreams, you start to gain momentum without even realizing it because, subconsciously, you've already put yourself into motion, starting with your mindset.

It's really not about talent because everyone has talent. It's the courage to try, to ask yourself, "What if?" That is the essence of manifesting your dreams.

Reflecting on all these experiences, I've realized every single "What if" has the potential to become my reality. Each dream I've manifested started with a simple thought, a flicker of possibility. It's a testament to the power of visualization and the courage to take that first step.

What about you? What dreams have you been quietly nurturing? What "What ifs" have you been afraid to voice? It's time to bring them to life. Start by imagining them vividly, feeling the excitement as if they've already come true. Trust in your vision, take that leap of faith, and watch as your dreams unfold.

Remember, it's not just about achieving your dreams; it's about the journey and the growth that comes with it. It's about embracing every moment along the way to manifesting your dreams. This is your journey, your story, and your chance to make your "What ifs" real. This is your journey to manifesting your dreams.

## WHAT I LEARNED

If you can dream it, you can become it.

Dreaming is not just a passive act of wishful thinking; it's the first step toward actualizing your deepest desires and aspirations. It's about daring to see beyond your current reality and envisioning the extraordinary possibilities that lie ahead. When you allow yourself to dream, you ignite a spark within that can illuminate your path, even in the darkest of times.

Dreams are the blueprint for your future. They are the seeds of potential that, with nurturing and dedication, can grow into remarkable achievements. But it's not enough to simply dream. You need to believe in your dreams with unwavering conviction. This belief fuels your actions, guiding you toward making your dreams a reality.

The power of visualization is one of the most profound lessons I learned. When you can vividly see yourself achieving your dreams, you begin to align your actions with your vision. Your subconscious starts to work toward making that vision come true, attracting opportunities and resources that support your journey. It's like your mind becomes a magnet, drawing in everything you need to succeed.

But dreaming alone isn't enough. It requires courage, resilience, and relentless effort. It's about pushing through the doubts, the fears, and the naysayers. It's about staying committed, even when the path gets tough and the goal seems distant. Your dreams demand you step out of your comfort zone, take risks, and embrace the unknown.

In my journey, I've faced numerous challenges and setbacks. Sometimes the dream seemed out of reach and the obstacles insurmountable. But I held on to my vision, believing if I could dream it, I could become it. Each step forward, no matter how small, brought me closer to my dreams. Every performance, every tour, every new opportunity was a testament to the power of dreaming big and working tirelessly toward those dreams.

What I've come to realize is your dreams are not just about personal fulfillment; they are a gift to the world. When you pursue your dreams, you inspire others to do the same. You show them it's possible to break free from limitations and live a life of purpose and passion. Your journey becomes a beacon of hope, lighting the way for others to follow.

So, what dreams are you holding in your heart? What vision do you have for your life? Remember, if you can dream it, you can become it. Embrace your dreams with all your heart, believe in them fiercely, and take the steps necessary to bring them to life. Your dreams are waiting for you to make them a reality. This is your time to shine, to rise, and to manifest the incredible future you envision.

Dream big, believe in yourself, and keep moving forward. The journey of fulfilling your dreams is not just about reaching the destination; it's about becoming the person you were always meant to be. Embrace the adventure, learn from every experience, and let your dreams guide you toward a life of fulfillment and joy. This is your journey of manifesting your dreams, and it starts with the courage to dream and the determination to make those dreams come true.

**EXERCISE**

1.  Are you dreaming a dream you're afraid to go after? Do you have a dream that scares you, makes you uncomfortable, or maybe makes you feel you're not good enough?

    - Activity: Write down your dream in detail. Describe why it scares you and what aspects make you feel uncomfortable or not good enough. Reflect on these feelings and consider how you can begin to overcome them.

    - Reflection: What small steps can you take to build confidence and reduce fear? How can you reframe your thoughts to view this dream as achievable?

_____

_____

_____

_____

_____

_____

_____

_____

_____

_____

_____

_____

_____

_____

_____

_____

_____

_____

2. What if you already accomplished your dream? How would it feel?

- Activity: Close your eyes and vividly imagine achieving your dream. Feel the emotions that come with this accomplishment. Write down these feelings and describe the scenario in as much detail as possible.

- Reflection: How do these feelings motivate you? How can you use this positive energy to fuel your actions toward achieving your dream?

_____

_____

_____

_____

_____

_____

3. What steps can you take today to bring your dreams closer to reality?

- Activity: List three specific actions you can take today to move closer to your dream. These could be small steps like researching, reaching out to someone, or practicing a skill.

- Reflection: How do these actions align with your overall goal? What influence do they have on your progress?

_____

_____

_____

_____

4.  What positive affirmations can you incorporate into your daily routine to reinforce your belief in your dreams?

    *   Activity: Create a list of positive affirmations that resonate with you and your dreams. Write them down and place them somewhere you'll see them daily, such as on your mirror or desk.

    *   Reflection: How do these affirmations influence your mindset and actions? How can you incorporate them into your daily routine effectively?

    _____

    _____

    _____

    _____

    _____

    _____

    _____

    _____

    _____

    _____

    _____

    _____

## FIVE TIPS FOR MANIFESTING YOUR DREAMS

1. **Visualize Your Dreams:** Take the time to vividly imagine your goals and aspirations as if they have already come to fruition. Allow yourself to feel the emotions associated with achieving those dreams.

2. **Set Clear Intentions:** Clearly and specifically define your dreams. Write them down, create vision boards, or share them with someone you trust. By articulating your desires clearly, you set the stage for manifesting them.

3. **Embrace Positive Affirmations:** Cultivate a mindset of belief and positivity by affirming your dreams daily. Use empowering statements that reinforce your ability to achieve your goals.

4. **Take Inspired Action:** Actively pursue your dreams by taking intentional steps toward realizing them. Break down your goals into manageable tasks and consistently work toward them with dedication and perseverance.

5. **Trust the Process:** Have faith in the journey and trust everything unfolds in divine timing. Release attachment to specific outcomes and remain open to unexpected opportunities and possibilities.

## SUMMARY

I've learned the power of visualization, intention-setting, positive affirmations, inspired action, and trust in the process of turning aspirations into reality. From performing with my musical idols to achieving career milestones and venturing into new endeavors, I've witnessed firsthand the transformative potential of manifesting dreams through focused thought and action.

I've also discovered fear and self-doubt can hinder the pursuit of dreams, creating barriers to success. Fear is a natural response to stepping into the unknown. It's a sign you're pushing your boundaries and reaching for something greater. Instead of letting fear paralyze you, use it as a signal you're on the right path. Self-doubt is another common obstacle. The key to overcoming self-doubt is recognizing it's just a thought, not a fact. Always challenge these negative beliefs. Know if you can dream it, you can become it. Your dreams are waiting for you to bring them to life.

Manifesting dreams requires a winning mindset. Cultivating this mindset involves determination and a positive attitude. Next, let's delve into the mindset needed for success.

## CALL TO ACTION

I challenge you to reflect on your dreams and aspirations. Are any fears or doubts holding you back from pursuing them? Identify one small step you can take today to overcome these barriers and move closer to realizing your dreams. It could be as simple as writing down your goals, reaching out to a mentor, or dedicating a few minutes each day to practicing a new skill.

www.DerickSebastian.com

# CHAPTER 21

# CULTIVATING YOUR WINNING MINDSET— "IT'S ON"

"Whatever the mind can conceive and believe, it can achieve."

— Napoleon Hill

**W**hat dreams have you allowed to fade because they seemed too big or out of reach? How often do you stop yourself from pursuing something because of fear or doubt? What if you dared to ask, "What if?" and took that first step toward your goal? As you reflect on your journey, think about the beliefs and thoughts that shaped your actions. Are they empowering you or holding you back? How can you begin to shift your mindset to one that propels you forward, turning your dreams into reality?

## MY STORY

In 2020, as the world stood still, I vowed not to conform to what was happening around me. Although all my gigs were canceled or postponed, I made a conscious decision to push forward and evolve as an artist. At first, I thought about simply writing and composing more music. Then, I stumbled upon Kris Bradley's *Produce Like a Boss* online course, which simplified the process of arranging, recording, and producing music—and even getting paid for it.

*Wait, what? Get paid for producing music?* I thought. My next question was, "How can I be unique, produce ukulele music, and actually get paid for it?"

The challenge was on, and *Produce Like a Boss* became a complete game-changer for me. Not only did I evolve as a songwriter, composer, and producer, but I also transformed into a creative entrepreneur.

I dove headfirst into the world of production music, writing compositions for film, television, advertisements, and media. Kris Bradley wasn't just an online mentor—she became a great friend and connected me with her incredible network of resources, including Gabriel Candiani of *Production Music Masterclass*, another game-changing online course.

Encouraged by this, I started reaching out to other resources on my own and soon found myself working with established music supervisors and major music libraries, which represent large catalogs of music for sync licensing.

The pressure was unlike anything I had experienced before. My first major project was to write, record, and produce a five-song album in just four weeks. I freaked out, but somehow, I pulled through. To my surprise, not only did I meet the deadline, but the project was good enough to be signed by Warner Chappell PM, an established music library.

The second major project I was assigned to was to write, record, and produce a ten-song album in four weeks. I honestly thought there was no way I could pull this off, but after breaking things down with detailed planning and precise discipline, I met the deadline, and this too was signed by Warner Chappell PM.

Then, when I thought it couldn't get any more difficult, I was assigned to produce a ten-song ukulele instrumental Christmas album in four weeks. What made it worse was I still needed to learn all the songs, note for note, with all the correct chords, and be on point with all the melodies and arrangements. And mind you, I do not read music—everything I do is by ear, patterns, and techniques. Again, I completely freaked out, which may have opened me up to a few anxiety attacks.

Despite the odds, I planned out the month in detail. My goal was to create a rigorous routine: one day to learn a Christmas song, followed by a day and a half to arrange, produce, and record it—including post-production. By sticking to this schedule for the entire month, I knew I could accomplish my goal. With drive, determination, and a non-negotiable commitment, the project was completed and signed to another major music library, Sky Urbano. Honestly, this Christmas album has become one of my favorite projects ever.

Throughout my life, I've faced challenges that required me to turn sour lemons into sweet lemonade. However, amid every trial, I've held onto the profound wisdom instilled in me by my late mentor and father figure, Mr.

Sam Ellis. He imparted invaluable lessons, emphasizing the power of belief and determination. "If you believe, you can do anything," he'd say. That mantra has echoed in my heart. Together, we dared to dream beyond the confines of our realities, dared to ask, "What if?" What began as whimsical musings soon evolved into tangible aspirations.

With each shared dream, we embarked on a journey fueled by excitement and passion, celebrating small victories that paved the way for greater achievements. Our bond grew stronger as we embraced the mantra, "It's On," a testament to our unwavering commitment to turn our dreams into reality. Though he may no longer live beside me, Mr. Ellis's spirit lives within me, guiding me as I continue to pursue my dreams with resilience, courage, and unwavering determination.

Stepping out of your comfort circle is the key to truly experiencing success. That doesn't necessarily mean becoming rich and famous, unless that's what you truly desire. What I mean is achieving what you set your mind to. For example, if you're a baseball player and your desire is to hit a home run, you most likely won't hit a home run your first time at bat. You will probably go through a series of disappointments.

Maybe you'll strike out, or perhaps just hit a single or two. Eventually, you'll start hitting doubles and triples. You might even fall back into a hitting slump—a rollercoaster of ups and downs. Then one day, after relentlessly showing up at the plate, it finally happens. You hit your first home run. Success is about setting goals beyond your comfort circle—small, reachable goals. When you achieve a small goal, set another one and achieve that too. This, my friend, is the true definition of success: putting your mind to something, believing it, and not giving up until you accomplish it.

Life often throws curveballs that can knock us off our feet. These are the moments when our mindset is crucial. It's easy to get discouraged, to let fear and doubt creep in, but the ones who succeed are the ones who push past these barriers. They understand failure is not the opposite of success; it's a part of it. Each setback is a setup for a comeback. This realization is what separates those who merely daydream from those who achieve their daydreams.

This is my secret to finding inner motivation, my "IT'S ON" method:

- **INSPIRED:** Infuse your spirit with boundless excitement, surround yourself with great relationships, and clearly envision success. Nurture synchronicities, pioneer innovation, radiate empowerment, and drive toward triumph. Inspiration is the fuel that keeps the fire of passion burning bright. When you feel inspired, everything seems possible. That spark ignites your drive and propels you forward, even when the path gets tough.

- **TALENT:** Trust in the brilliance of your unique gifts, the essence of your greatness. Activate your potential through bold action, lead with relentless enthusiasm, nurture creativity, and transform lives with purpose. Recognize your talent is a gift meant to be shared with the world. It's not about being the best; it's about being the best you. Use your talents to make a difference, to inspire others, and to fulfill your purpose.

- **SHINE:** Summon the courage to radiate brilliance, illuminating the path ahead. Harness your plans, fortify resilience, seek wisdom, and soar toward your goals with unwavering determination. Shining is about stepping into your power, embracing your strengths, and letting your light guide you and others. It's about being confident in who you are and what you have to offer.

- **O**WN: Embrace your whole being, stand firmly in your truth, and embrace the journey of your evolution. Overcome obstacles with resilience, navigating the unknown with grace and confidence. Owning your journey means taking responsibility for your actions, your growth, and your success. It's about being authentic, staying true to your values, and owning your story.

- **N**EVER GIVE UP: Navigate the journey with unyielding resolve, embodying the essence of perseverance. Emerge victorious through every trial, embodying tenacity and unwavering determination. Rise stronger with each fall—victory awaits the resilient soul. Persistence is the key to achieving anything worthwhile. It's about pushing through the pain, the setbacks, and the failures. It's about having the grit to keep going no matter what.

Minding your mindset is crucial. When you adopt the "It's On" attitude, you arm yourself with the tools to face any challenge head-on. This mindset is about staying inspired, trusting your talent, shining brightly, owning your journey, and never giving up. This mindset transforms obstacles into opportunities and setbacks into setups for a greater comeback. Embrace the "It's On" mentality and watch as you bring your aspirations to life.

In life's journey, mindset is your compass. It directs you toward your goals and helps you navigate the storms. A positive, resilient mindset doesn't just happen; it's cultivated through practice and perseverance. By focusing on the "It's On" principles, you equip yourself with the resilience and determination needed to turn your dreams into accomplishments.

So, whenever you face a challenge, remember to say, "It's On." Embrace the journey with all its ups and downs and keep pushing forward. Your dreams are within reach if you believe, remain determined, and keep your mindset strong. This is the essence of manifesting your dreams and minding your mindset—embracing every moment, learning from every experience, and knowing you have the power to shape your destiny.

## WHAT I LEARNED

Everything starts in the mind. Change your thoughts, and you change your words. Change your words, and you change your actions—and your reality.

Our thoughts shape our perceptions and guide our actions. The mindset we choose can be our greatest ally or our biggest obstacle. The mind is where dreams are born and fears take root. By nurturing positive thoughts, we create space for growth and success.

Changing your mindset begins with self-awareness—recognizing negative patterns and limiting beliefs. Often, we sabotage ourselves with doubt and fear. But once we identify these roadblocks, we can transform them into self-belief, courage, and action.

One of the most powerful tools I've learned is the practice of positive affirmations and visualization. When you consistently tell yourself that you're capable and deserving, you start to believe it. Visualize your goals as if they're already achieved, aligning your actions with your aspirations.

Setting clear intentions is key. Intentions act as a roadmap, keeping you focused and motivated. They remind you of your *why* and help you stay committed when the journey gets tough.

Taking action is just as important. It's not enough to think positively—you must back it with purposeful steps. Each small action creates momentum and moves you closer to your dreams.

Trust the process. Progress may seem slow, and the path may be unclear, but faith in the journey will keep you grounded. Every effort and challenge is part of the bigger picture.

Are fears or doubts holding you back? Take one small step today to move closer to your dreams. Remember, your mindset is the key to unlocking a future of endless possibilities. Changing your mind is a continuous practice, but it's worth it. When you change your mindset, you change your life.

It's on.

**EXERCISE**

1.  Have you ever had to adopt a non-negotiable "IT'S ON" mindset?

    *   Activity: Reflect on a significant moment when you had to embrace an "IT'S ON" mindset. Write about the situation, your feelings, the actions you took, and the outcome.

    *   Reflection: How did mindset help you overcome challenges? What lessons did you take away from this experience?

_____

_____

_____

_____

2.  Who inspires you, and how can you connect with them for motivation?

    - Activity: Identify three people or communities who inspire you. Explore ways to connect with them, such as through social media, events, or online platforms.

    - Reflection: How can these connections support your journey? What steps will you take to engage with these inspiring people or groups?

    _____

    _____

    _____

    _____

3.  What are your greatest strengths, and how can you leverage them to achieve your goals?

    - Activity: List your top five strengths and talents. Consider specific ways you can use these strengths to reach your goals and make the world a better place.

- Reflection: How can you incorporate these strengths into your daily routine? What new opportunities can you explore to maximize your talents?

 

 

 

 

4. How do you currently cultivate resilience, and how can you further develop this practice?

- Activity: Write down your current methods for building resilience. Identify one new practice or habit that can enhance your resilience and wisdom.

- Reflection: How have these practices helped you in the past? How can you integrate new practices into your life to further strengthen your resilience?

 

 

 

 

## FIVE TIPS FOR TURNING ON YOUR "IT'S ON" MINDSET

1. **Surround Yourself with Inspiration:** Actively seek out people who share your passions and goals, and engage in experiences that fuel your enthusiasm and motivation. Attend workshops, join communities, and build relationships with people who inspire and support your dreams.

2. **Leverage Your Talents:** Identify your unique strengths and talents, and find ways to use them to propel yourself forward. Whether it's through honing your skills, taking on new challenges, or sharing your expertise with others, lead with enthusiasm and a clear sense of purpose in everything you do.

3. **Fortify Resilience and Seek Wisdom:** Strengthen resilience by cultivating a growth mindset and learning from both successes and failures. Seek wisdom from mentors, books, and life experiences, and use these insights to navigate challenges with determination and grace.

4. **Embrace Ownership:** Take ownership of your journey and embrace every aspect of your personal growth and evolution. Recognize you have the power to shape your destiny, and approach each obstacle as an opportunity to learn and develop.

5. **Never Give Up:** Adopt an unwavering resolve to persevere through every trial and setback. Draw strength from your resilience and inner determination, knowing each challenge you overcome makes you stronger and brings you closer to achieving your dreams.

## SUMMARY

In this chapter, I delved into the mindset needed to turn aspirations into reality, drawing inspiration from my mentor, Mr. Sam Ellis, and his wisdom. I introduced the "IT'S ON" method and outlined its five key strategies for achieving our dreams: surrounding yourself with inspiration, leveraging your talents, fortifying resilience, embracing ownership, and never giving up. Each strategy emphasizes the importance of mindset, determination, and personal growth in pursuing goals. Surrounding yourself with inspiration involves seeking out positive influences and maintaining a clear vision of success. By embodying these principles, you can navigate challenges with resilience, draw strength from setbacks, and ultimately, emerge victorious in your endeavors.

Remember, everything starts within your mind. Change your mind and you change your life. Embrace the power of your mindset—it's on!

A winning mindset sets the stage for purposeful daydreaming. Turning dreams into reality through intention and focus is the culmination of our journey. Now let's bring it all together in the final chapter.

## CALL TO ACTION

I challenge you to examine your current mindset. Are you surrounding yourself with the right inspiration and fully leveraging your talents? Identify one key area where you can make a shift today, whether it's fortifying your resilience or committing to trying something new. Remember, when life knocks you down, you must get back up again. Embrace the "IT'S ON" mindset, knowing a setback is just a setup for a comeback. This is your moment—transform your aspirations into reality. What will you do to ignite this change? Remember, everything starts in your mind. Embrace this power—it's on!

www.DerickSebastian.com

# CHAPTER 22

# YOUR DAYDREAMING WITH PURPOSE

"Dreams are illustrations from the book your soul is writing about you."

— Marsha Norman

Which dreams have you quietly nurtured but never fully pursued? What if you gave yourself permission to explore those dreams, to let your imagination run wild, and to believe they are within reach? What if the only thing holding you back is the fear of taking that first step? As you read on, consider how your own daydreams might lead to your greatest achievements—if you dare to follow them. What are your passions? What is your purpose? How can you turn those passions into your profession so you can live out your purpose?

**MY STORY**

Being the youngest child of four, I grew up observing a lot, especially my older siblings. I wasn't outspoken and didn't have the personality to make myself known. I was quiet, but I did one thing a lot: I whispered to myself. For some reason, I would quietly repeat to myself phrases I heard people use or whatever sounded interesting to me. I did this a lot. Everyone around me would say, "Derick, why are you repeating yourself?" At first, I was a little ashamed of it, questioning, "Why do I repeat myself? Is something wrong with me?" But truthfully, it didn't really bother me. I was comfortable with it.

As I got older, especially in high school, I found myself talking to myself more—sometimes out loud, but mostly in my mind. As strange as it may sound, I'd have conversations in my head, almost as if there were two versions of me. I found comfort in being alone. I didn't belong to a specific clique of friends; instead, I had many friends and would roam around during recess and lunch, just going with the flow. Sometimes I'd hang out in classrooms, the cafeteria, or the library. Other times, I'd be playing ukulele with my cool music friends in the hallways, or I'd find myself completely content and alone in the music studio, just recording or writing.

It's funny, I know, but this ultimately led to something I did well: daydreaming. Now I've learned some of the most intelligent people in the world internally talk to themselves a lot. It's just a way for the brain to communicate with the soul. Many never understand this, but it's a good thing.

I found it fascinating to envision myself doing things that seemed "Way out of my reach" or impossible. As a little kid, I daydreamed about flying and becoming a pilot because I loved airplanes. Then I discovered playing baseball, and I daydreamed about making it to the major leagues, which really got me excited. Eventually, I discovered the ukulele, and from there, I daydreamed about how amazing it would be to play my ukulele around the world. Sometimes, I daydreamed about being so successful it scared me. The imposter syndrome always lingered behind me: Who am I to think this? I'm not good enough; I'm just a teenage kid dreaming his life away. But somehow, someway, I found the little mustard seed of hope and belief that I had the power to become whatever I wanted to be.

I daydreamed about performing ukulele locally at Maui restaurants, hotels, and music clubs. Done!

I daydreamed about collaborating and being the opening act on big stages for major established artists from around the world. Done!

I daydreamed about recording an ukulele instrumental album and having it nominated at the Na Hoku Hanohano Awards. Done!

I daydreamed about traveling the world, inspiring others through touring and teaching the ukulele. This brought me across the US, Australia, Thailand, the Philippines, South Korea, China, Canada, Germany, Finland, and Estonia. Done!

I daydreamed about performing for NCAA events, which led me to perform for the Maui Invitational Men's Basketball Tournament and Maui Classic Women's Basketball Tournament, allowing me to work with multiple Division One schools, especially Oregon State University. Done!

I daydreamed about making history and breaking into major sporting events by performing the national anthem on my ukulele, which led me to perform at multiple stadiums, arenas, and golf courses, working with numerous professional sports teams in the MLB, NBA, PGA, and ESPN. Done!

I daydreamed about becoming a speaker at TEDx, and it happened at TEDx Santa Cruz. Done!

I daydreamed about connecting with and performing for major television and movie companies, which led me to perform for ABC's *Grey's Anatomy* and Pixar Animation Studios. Done!

I daydreamed about establishing an ukulele program on Maui at a high-end resort, and it happened at the Andaz Maui at Wailea Resort. Done!

I daydreamed about becoming an established wedding musician and officiant. Done!

I daydreamed about becoming a songwriter, composer, and producer, releasing my own music, and writing for licensing, production libraries, TV, commercials, and ads. Done!

I daydreamed about having my original music signed by major music libraries and companies, which led me to being signed by Warner Chappell PM, Sky Urbano, Atrium Music, Hyatt Worldwide, and ROXY Quicksilver. Done!

I daydreamed about writing my own book and becoming an author. Done!

I am now daydreaming about expanding to inspire others not just in music but also as a professional keynote speaker, coach, and creative entrepreneur. I'm on my way and so excited about this new journey.

Give yourself permission to dream, envision, and say yes to whatever comes to you. Usually, what stops us isn't necessarily about our capabilities or gifts. Everyone is born with a gift, a purpose bigger than themselves. It's really up to us to respond to our calling and accept the challenges and discomfort. The one thing every human struggles with is fear. Fear of what others may think, fear of not being good enough, or the main reason people don't even try, fear of failing.

As the legendary singer and songwriter John Mayer once said, "Don't ever kill the idea when you haven't even tried. You need to allow yourself to try and see what happens; from there, you learn and find your way."

Life isn't just about being alive; you need to live! You need to grow, flourish, and be curious enough to see where you belong. You're unique, and whether you believe it or not, there is a space specifically for you and your gift. Life is a journey, and every so often, you need to be courageous enough to lift up each steppingstone in front of you and see what's beneath it. Everything you find may not be for you, but some surely will. Every stone is an opportunity. Yes, you may fail, but the truth is, there is no failure—it's all lessons learned. Every single failure is beneficial for you, and only you.

When you are tested, you grow. And when you grow, you gain knowledge, and ultimately, wisdom. Don't let yourself craft excuses to convince yourself to stay where you are. Leap into the unknown and grow into who you really are. Know you're powerful and already good enough, no permission needed. Free your heart to follow your joy and discover your true purpose and abundant life. Don't think stepping out of your comfort zone is too risky. The truth is, being alive is risky. Allow yourself to experience what your heart desires, and you'll find your way. You get one chance to live your life to the fullest, so do it!

Use your words carefully because what comes out of your mouth comes into your life.

This is the essence of your daydreaming with purpose.

## WHAT I LEARNED

Daydreaming is far more powerful than most people think. In fact, everyone daydreams, but it usually stops there. The key difference is when you daydream with purpose, you find yourself gravitating toward actions that make your dreams come true. Your mind becomes the driving force, turning your thoughts into actions.

Purposeful daydreaming transforms idle fantasies into achievable goals. It provides a mental blueprint to guide your actions, helping you visualize success and map out the steps needed to reach your dream. When you daydream with intent, you are not just imagining a distant possibility; you are rehearsing for reality. This mental rehearsal prepares you for the actual journey, making you more confident and ready to seize opportunities as they arise.

As I reflect on my journey, I realize every significant milestone began as a daydream. Visualizing myself performing on grand stages or collaborating with renowned artists was the first step. These dreams fueled my determination and provided the motivation to pursue them relentlessly. I found myself taking small but consistent steps toward these visions, whether it was practicing tirelessly, seeking out gigs, or networking with industry professionals.

Purposeful daydreaming also helps overcome obstacles. When you have a clear vision of what you want to achieve, you are more likely to persist through challenges and setbacks. You understand these hurdles are part of the process, and you are willing to navigate them because the goal is always in sight. The mindset shift from mere dreaming to purposeful visualization is crucial in turning aspirations into achievements.

Moreover, daydreaming with purpose opens your mind to endless possibilities. It encourages creative thinking and problem solving, allowing you to see opportunities where others might see barriers. It fosters resilience, as you continuously adapt your strategies and stay focused on your goals despite the odds.

In my musical journey, purposeful daydreaming has been a cornerstone of my success. It has guided me through the highs and lows, keeping me focused on my ultimate goals. Every performance, every gig, and every collaboration started as a dream, but with intention and action, they became my reality.

**EXERCISE**

1.  Are you daydreaming with purpose?

    •   Activity: Think about your current daydreams. Write down the ones that excite you the most and evaluate if they reflect daydreaming with intent and purpose.

    •   Reflection: How can you shift these daydreams into purposeful visions that drive you toward specific actions and goals?

_____

_____

_____

2. How can you turn your internal monologue into a supportive voice guiding you toward your dreams?

- Activity: Identify negative or doubtful thoughts that frequently arise in your internal dialogue. Write them down and then transform each into a positive affirmation.

- Reflection: How can you regularly practice these positive affirmations to build a supportive internal monologue?

_____

_____

_____

_____

_____

3. What specific achievement can you visualize today? What does it look like in vivid detail?

- Activity: Choose one significant goal or dream. Write a detailed description of what achieving this goal looks like, including sights, sounds, emotions, and the environment.

- Reflection: How does visualizing this achievement make you feel? What steps can you take to move closer to this vision?

_____

_____

_____

_____

_____

_____

4. What small success can you achieve this week to prove to yourself your dreams are valid?

- Activity: Identify a small, achievable goal related to your larger dreams. Make a plan to accomplish it within the week.

- Reflection: How does achieving this small success enhance your confidence and provide motivation to pursue bigger dreams?

_____

_____

_____

_____

_____

_____

## FIVE TIPS FOR DAYDREAMING WITH PURPOSE

1. **Embrace Your Inner Voice:** When I was growing up, the habit of whispering phrases to myself helped shape my internal dialogue and vision. Embracing this inner voice allowed me to craft a personal narrative that aligns with my dreams.

2. **Visualize Specific Achievements:** Much like the detailed daydreams that led to performing at major events and creating music internationally, visualizing specific goals can make them feel more attainable and real.

3. **Challenge Self-Doubt with Small Successes:** Your journey shows how small achievements validate your dreams and build confidence, helping to overcome imposter syndrome.

4. **Use Daydreams as a Blueprint:** Daydreams served as blueprints for my actions, from playing the ukulele globally to teaching and speaking. Viewing daydreams as plans rather than just fantasies can propel you to action.

5. **Expand Your Comfort Zone:** I've seen how expanding daydreams to include seemingly unreachable goals can stretch my abilities and reveal hidden potential.

## SUMMARY

In this chapter, I delved into the transformative power of purposeful daydreaming. As the youngest child, I nurtured my dreams in solitude, gradually turning them from whispers into actions that shaped my reality. This chapter illustrates how specific visions, deliberate planning, and overcoming self-doubt lead to success. Daydreaming involves not only dreaming big but taking concrete steps to manifest these dreams, challenging oneself to expand beyond familiar limits. Purposeful daydreaming helps transform idle fantasies into achievable goals. By fostering a mindset where thoughts inspire emotions that drive actions, daydreaming becomes a powerful tool for creating our reality.

I encourage you to identify your deepest dreams and initiate the journey toward them, pushing past fears and embracing the full potential of your life's purpose. Let your daydreams be more than fleeting thoughts; use them as a roadmap to guide your actions and bring your visions to life.

## CALL TO ACTION

I challenge you to take your daydreams from mere thoughts to actionable plans. Identify one dream you've held close and ask yourself: What steps can I take today to start making this dream a reality? Push past the fears that hold you back and embrace the potential within. Let your daydreams be the blueprint for success, guiding your every action toward fulfilling your life's purpose. Remember, every great achievement starts with a single, daring thought—turn your daydreams into your roadmap for success.

Embrace your daydreams with purpose. Let them be more than fleeting thoughts. Use them as tools to envision and build your future, motivate yourself, and guide your actions. It's not just about dreaming; it's about turning those dreams into reality through consistent effort and unwavering belief.

www.DerickSebastian.com

# A FINAL NOTE

# LIVING ALOHA

"The journey of a thousand miles begins with one step."

— Lao Tzu

Now that you've read my book, what are you going to do? What goals are you going to set? Which hidden dreams need to come forward? Which relationships do you need to work on? What changes are you going to make?

I challenge you to act! Knowledge alone isn't power; the application of knowledge is what truly makes a difference. You can read every self-help book out there, but if you don't take the wisdom from this book and use it in your daily life, you'll stay right where you are.

The ten exercise prompts below are the ten actions I challenge you to commit to taking within the next ninety days as a result of reading this book:

1. **Identify Your Purpose:** Spend time each day reflecting on your true passions and goals. Write down what drives you and what you want to

achieve. Create a vision board that visually represents your dreams and keep it where you can see it daily.

_____

_____

_____

_____

2. **Set Clear Goals:** Outline specific, actionable goals for the next ninety days. Break them down into smaller, manageable tasks and set deadlines for each. Track your progress and celebrate small victories along the way.

_____

_____

_____

_____

3. **Overcome Fear:** Identify one fear that has been holding you back. Challenge yourself to take a step toward overcoming it. This could be making a difficult phone call, starting a new project, or speaking up in a situation where you usually stay silent.

_____

_____

_____

_____

4.  **Practice Forgiveness:** Reflect on any grudges or unresolved conflicts. Write a letter of forgiveness to yourself or someone else, even if you don't send it. Let go of the negative emotions associated with these conflicts.

    _____

    _____

    _____

    _____

5.  **Daydream with Purpose:** Dedicate time each week to intentional daydreaming. Visualize success, imagine future achievements, and let your mind explore new possibilities. Write down these daydreams and identify actionable steps to make them a reality.

    _____

    _____

    _____

    _____

6.  **Take Daily Action:** Commit to taking at least one action that moves you closer to your goals every day. It can be a small step, like sending an email, or a big one, like completing a project milestone. Consistency is key.

    _____

    _____

    _____

    _____

7.  **Embrace Rejection:** Reframe your perspective on rejection. For the next ninety days, seek opportunities where you might face rejection. Use these experiences to learn and grow. Remember, rejection is just redirection.

 

_____

_____

_____

_____

8.  **Strengthen Relationships:** Identify key relationships in need of nurturing. Spend time with these people, have meaningful conversations, and express your appreciation for them. Building strong connections will support your journey.

 

_____

_____

_____

_____

9.  **Cultivate Gratitude:** Start a gratitude journal. Each day, write down at least three things you are grateful for. This practice will help you focus on the positive aspects of your life and maintain a positive mindset.

 

_____

_____

_____

_____

10. **Live Authentically:** Assess areas where you might be conforming to others' expectations rather than being true to yourself. Make a conscious effort to align your actions with your values and desires. Be unapologetically you.

_____

_____

_____

_____

In this book, you learned about the transformative power of following your passions and embracing your unique journey. You explored themes of overcoming fear, practicing forgiveness, and persisting through challenges with a resilient spirit. You discovered the importance of daydreaming with purpose, owning your regrets, and finding your true _why_. Through my personal stories and insights, you learned how to navigate life's unpredictability, cultivate meaningful relationships, and live authentically. This book showed you that true success is not measured by accolades or material wealth but by the joy and fulfillment found in living a life that aligns with your deepest values and purpose.

If you apply the wisdom, knowledge, experience, skills, strategies, and techniques offered in this book, you will achieve and find your way through your daydreaming with purpose.

Now that you've finished my book, I'd love to hear from you. Let me know what resonated with you and what didn't so I can improve future editions.

But more importantly, I want to hear your story—your challenges, obstacles, and adversity—so we can work together to find ways to overcome them.

If my book has inspired you or brought value to your life, it would mean the world to me if you could leave a review wherever you purchased it. Reviews are incredibly important for authors like myself because they help others discover the book and ensure that I can continue sharing these messages with a wider audience. Your thoughts and feedback are truly appreciated and will make a significant difference.

Please feel free to reach out to me at Team@DerickSebastian.com. From the bottom of my heart, thank you so much for your time and for being part of my journey. I sincerely wish you all the success and prosperity in the world.

As you step forward, remember the essence of Living Aloha. It's about embracing life with love, compassion, and kindness. It's about acting on your dreams, nurturing relationships, and living authentically. By incorporating the Spirit of Aloha into your daily life, you can create a ripple effect of positivity and transformation. Let's embark on this journey together, living each day with purpose and joy.

One last challenge for you, my friend: I challenge you to let the "Aloha Spirit" fill your breath and your soul, and let it shine for the world to see! One of the best ways to do this is by developing your own talents and sharing them with the world, just as I have done with my life.

So, I challenge you to pick up an ukulele, get some lessons, and play it every day! If the uke isn't your thing, then try the guitar, piano, or even take singing lessons. Maybe drums are your thing. Whatever it is, deep inside, you already know what your passions are. And when you develop them, greatness will follow. Be brave enough to be a beginner. You are a legend in the making, so never quit. Don't let anyone tell you otherwise. If I can become a musician, songwriter, composer, producer, and now an author, so can you!

The world is waiting for your gifts. Don't play small—go big and make God proud of the talents He's given you. This is my challenge to you. If you practice every day like I have, you too can turn your passions into your profession!

Mahalo and Aloha! I believe in you.

Now is your time! Let's go!

It's on! Automatic!

Derick Sebastian

www.DerickSebastian.com

# ABOUT THE AUTHOR

DERICK SEBASTIAN is an accomplished author, professional keynote speaker, life coach, singer, songwriter, producer, composer, and ukulele artist.

Born and raised in Maui, Derick embodies the Spirit of Aloha through perseverance and passion. As an international ukulele virtuoso, he has captured the hearts of fans worldwide, earning recognition as one of the greatest ukulele players in the world.

Derick has shared the stage with some of the industry's brightest stars, including Jason Mraz, Raining Jane, Trombone Shorty, and legendary Christian artists like Michael W. Smith, Natalie Grant, and Bernie Herms. He has also performed alongside country music icons such as Lukas Nelson, Lily Meola, Chris Young, Randy Houser, Mitchell Tenpenny, Kameron Marlowe, Thompson Square, and Sara Evans. The ukulele community embraces Derick as a fellow ace, and he has collaborated with Jake Shimabukuro and had memorable moments with R&B sensations Boyz II Men and Brian McKnight.

Derick's impressive journey has taken him to renowned venues like Crypto.com Arena, Dodger Stadium, Chase Field, Oracle Park, T-Mobile Park, and prestigious events such as TEDx Santa Cruz. His music has been featured in PIXAR Animation Studios productions, ABC's *Grey's Anatomy*, and within the realms of MLB, NBA, PGA, NCAA, ESPN, and EA SPORTS.

Through these experiences, Derick has honed his craft and embraced new creative ventures in songwriting, composing, and producing music for film, TV, and advertisements. His compositions for ROXY, Hyatt's global campaigns, and collaborations with major libraries like Warner Chappell PM, Sky Urbano, and Atrium Music demonstrate his expanding influence in the music industry.

Adding author now to his repertoire, Derick's debut book, *Daydreaming With Purpose*, is a self-help memoir that captures the essence of his life's lessons, dreams, and relationships. It reflects his unyielding spirit and dedication to inspiring others through his stories. Despite his challenges with asthma, allergies, eczema, gout, colorblindness, anxiety, and episodes of depression, Derick has fought to continue finding his vibration, following his intuition, and ultimately, finding ways to win at life.

Derick's narrative is one of resilience, illustrating how he navigated career challenges, overcame fears, and consistently pursued his passions. His commitment to his craft and his humility shine through in every endeavor, as he remains true to his roots and dedicated to inspiring others through music and writing. As a wedding virtuoso and author, Derick's multifaceted talents and unwavering dedication continue to make a positive difference in the world.

Connect with Derick Sebastian to follow his journey and be inspired by his music and life lessons:

Instagram: https://www.instagram.com/DerickSebastian

Facebook: https://www.facebook.com/DerickSebastianPage

LinkedIn: https://www.linkedin.com/in/DerickSebastian

Pinterest: https://www.pinterest.com/TheDerickSebastian

YouTube: https://www.youtube.com/c/DerickSebastian

Website: https://www.DerickSebastian.com

www.DerickSebastian.com

# ABOUT THE AUTHOR

## (IN HAWAIIAN PIDGIN LANGUAGE)

### THIS IS DERICK SEBASTIAN'S LIFE STORY

**Da Way He Talk'em, Da Way He Like You Read'em!**

"Be strong, know who you are, no be shame, stand up, e ala e (rise up)."

— Israel Kamakawiwo'ole

FROM BEFORE TIME, DEN JUST GEEVUM! (GO AFTER IT!)

Aloha and Howzit! Ho man, life can get crazy when you do what Bruddah Derick Sebastian stay do nowadays. Life is driven by his dreams and desires, and he get choke plenty [a lot of it!]. Some days he gotta just stop and reflect the early days of his life, his music, and his island roots. My Bruddah Derick, this Maui boy, born and raised. He no can even tell you how proud he stay, being raised on one beautiful island. The tropical vegetation, food, island people, and lifestyle, food...oh, he said that already! Eh, but the local food only ono [delicious] you know! Cruise kine life [easy living] and every place you look is nothing but paradise, choke [beyond amazing] nice! How much bettah (better) you can make your life even mo' bettah [more better]?

So in his early kine days, Derick had to grow up kinda fast. Because he had to, when he was raised by his mom. How sad that he lost his dad when he was only three years old. He tried for be the best kid for his mom, but he got kinda lost, no mo' faddah figgah [father figure] like most young boys. So small kid time [when he was young], Derick stay reach out to people in his life that he hope going be one good influence for him. Then he went meet that one man at one early age, Mr. Sam "Mistah" Ellis. Mistah Ellis, who was the school campus security guard and small kine counselor, went teach Derick plenty for reals [seriously]! Derick believe that Mistah Ellis was one faddah figgah he can look up to. Learning all kine life lessons and teach him how play ukulele, Mistah Ellis was one big influence in his young life! Now Derick hooked on da ukulele, was so unreal! He went get good fast learning from Mistah Ellis, but Derick was hungry for learn more to get mo' bettah! Mistah Ellis saw he had da kine [you know, like "special"] talent and knew he can be good so long he stay with it…just play, play, and play some more!

## AN' DEN, ANWHAT NEXT?

Fast forward kinda plenty, Derick stay learn all kine plenty and getting unreal good! He start winning ukulele contests and getting mo' bettah [more improved]! He was in demand and started playing local kine gigs around Maui, like Hula Grill and Duke's in Kaanapali, hotels and laddat [and so on] kine! Bruddah Derick went produce and release his CD, and went blow his mind! This album, *From His Heart*, had get voted in as finalist for Na Hoku Hanohano Award, the Grammys of Hawai'i! His ukulele skills was getting plenty recognition, so Derick went get ask for headline ukulele festivals. The blessings was coming, so he get to travel to America [US mainland]

and various international countries for display his skills now as one ukulele virtuoso, and also teach ukulele! Derick went get so good just like Mistah Ellis expected, he also get ask to showcase playing ukulele and meet unreal kine notable [amazing and well known] musicians call him up on stage for play. Then meet cool celebrities da kine you see on TV, all because one humble little instrument he was blessed to play and unreal good at it.

Then got to one point where Derick now gotta focus on the next important phase in his life…gotta be more for do? He ask himself what he must do for make one living playing music with the ukulele? This journey is all because he like provide for his *ohana* and do what he really love! Then one big question, "What that going take?" With the grace of Ke Akua [God], he got one call from one of the big wigs [management] of one nice Maui resort called Andaz Maui at Wailea for discuss the hotel's cultural program. Now look, they go assign Derick one long standing program at Andaz, teaching ukulele as one cultural practitioner. Not only that, he stay on one small kine priority vendor list performing choke [many, many] private events at Andaz!

Derick stay do so well, he get hired for choke plenty [many, many] weddings providing music services playing ukulele all over Hawaii! He then go figure out, he also can learn to be one wedding officiant too! So, the clients get choices now, they can get him for only music or get the whole package deal both da kine [you know] officiant and musician! Brah, he go, cuz! [Man, he get this going on!] So, Derick had to get licensed to be a wedding officiant, and he called his purpose as also spreading the "Language of Love." Now he stay really feel more accomplished…still, he like summoh! [I want more!] All that he doing getting way mo' bettah!

Derick was not pau doing all he wanted [he was not finished and wanted more], so he take one more big step and start taking online courses for be one mo' bettah [more accomplished] creative business man! Small kine [little bit] stressful and now plenty pressure to learn while he still balance everything with his ambitions and his family life. But remember, he get that drive with purpose to advance himself to do more, and be even mo' bettah!

He like keep climbing the opportunity ladder, so Derick went also learn big time in songwriting, composing, and production music. Take small kine couple years, but now his original music and compositions stay exposed on platforms for film, television, advertising, commercials, and media. How super-cool is that and choke [very, very] nice accomplishment! But check this out, he not only limited to the ukulele instrument, using his knowledge and skills with electronic music! Now all his creativity with his music stay get licensed with some big music libraries, working with some cherry [top-notch] music supervisors, directors, writers, and creatives! Not only that, he even create his own publishing company! Eh, you know what they say, yeah? You gotta go BIG, or you stay all pau! [all finished!]

## EH, NOT PAU YET...GET CHOKE MO' [SO MUCH MORE] FOR DO!

Derick's dreams go big, but he gotta...no can stop! Even with all this kine scary adventures, this is what make him develop into what he believe, "all in God's plan for him." So he still dream choke plenty! For reals! [Dream so much, really!] If you stop, then for what is your purpose? [Then what's the point?] The point is, Derick doing what he love and provide for family, his closest loved ones. With his lovely and supportive wife and their three sons he loves all dearly, how you no can? So, what is that big word? Persevere.

Turn the page to the next chapter in the Derick Sebastian journey. So now he like help you go big in your own life and be mo' bettah! He like help and teach others to do what he doing, so you no make the same mistakes. He can help guide you through with his knowledge and inspiration from his own experience. He like support and motivate others to realize their own dreams and make it all possible.... CAN YOU KNOW, CAN! [YOU CAN DO IT TOO!]

Days are long, life is short, and you only get one shot! You gotta go after your life with hard work, dedication, persistence, and with one mindset so strong, nothin' in this world going stop you! If you really believe, your dreams going become reality, no matter how hard going be! As for life, going just be, MO' BETTAH!

Bruddah Derick Sebastian walk his life the best way he know how, with simple Love and Aloha and with God at his side. Very humbly, he ask for you to join his mission. Together, Derick and you can make one difference in this world, one Aloha at a time!

— Written and Translated by Rick "Wikiboy" Rasay
Artist, Performer, and Creative Development Director

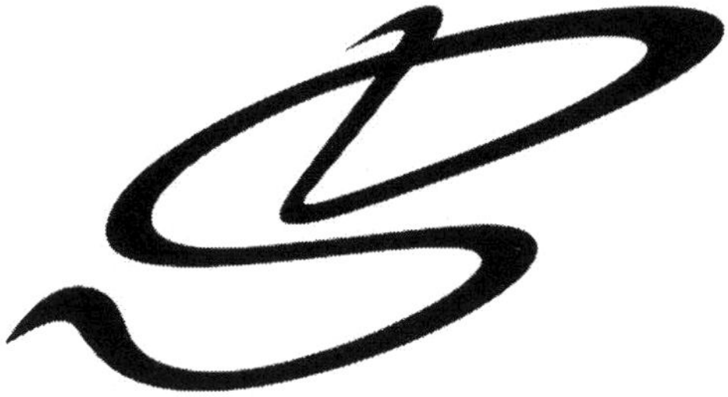

# ABOUT DERICK SEBASTIAN'S MUSIC AND CREATIVE OFFERINGS

Derick Sebastian is a trailblazing creative entrepreneur, constantly pushing boundaries and exploring new ways to express his gifts and talents, especially through his words and ukulele. He firmly believes art has the power to inspire, heal, and bring people together. Derick's music is at the heart of his story, reflecting his personal journey and blending his experiences with universal themes that resonate with listeners from all walks of life. His unique style and heartfelt performances captivate audiences, creating unforgettable moments and meaningful connections.

Here's a list of Derick's creative services:

**Live Performances for Private and Corporate Events:** Elevate your event with Derick's mesmerizing live performances.

**Ukulele National Anthem:** Add a unique and patriotic touch to your event with Derick's ukulele rendition of the national anthem.

**Music Licensing:** Hire Derick for songwriting and composing for television, film, advertisements, and media projects.

**Wedding Musician:** Create a magical atmosphere at your wedding with Derick's enchanting music.

**Wedding Officiant:** Let Derick officiate your wedding, sharing the "Language of Love" through word and music.

**Ukulele Lessons:** Learn to play the ukulele with personalized lessons from Derick himself.

Ready to bring the magic of Derick's music to your life? Connect with Derick and experience the transformative power of his music firsthand! To book a performance or lesson today, contact Derick at:

www.DerickSebastian.com

Team@DerickSebastian.com

(808) 870-8460

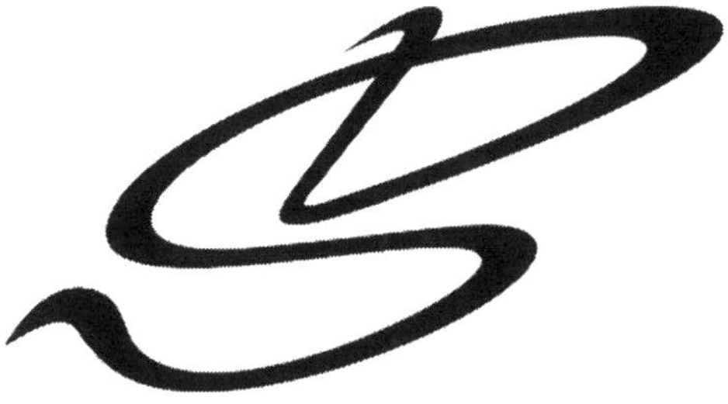

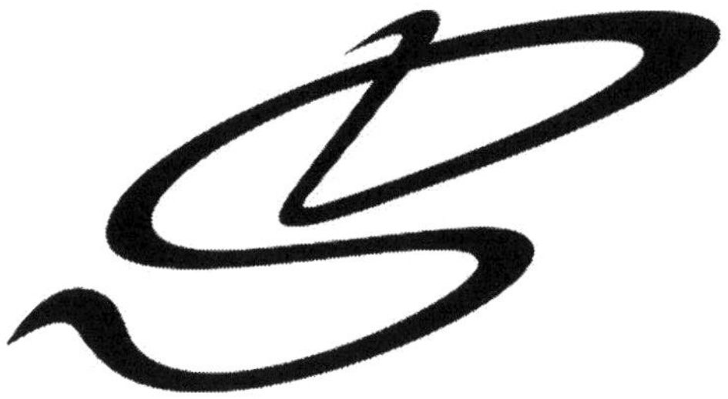

# ABOUT DERICK SEBASTIAN'S LIFE COACHING

As you've journeyed through this book, you've seen the transformative power of pursuing passions, overcoming challenges, and embracing life's unexpected twists and turns. Derick Sebastian's experiences have taught him invaluable lessons about resilience, creativity, and personal growth. Now, he is excited to offer you the opportunity to work with him directly through life coaching to unlock your full potential.

**Why Choose Life Coaching with Derick Sebastian?**

- **Personalized Guidance:** Benefit from tailored advice and strategies that align with your unique goals and challenges.

- **Empowerment:** Gain the confidence to pursue your passions and overcome obstacles with a resilient mindset.

- **Accountability:** Stay on track and motivated with regular check-ins and support.

- **Inspiration:** Draw from Derick's experiences and insights to unlock your full potential and live a fulfilling life.

Life Coaching Services:

- **One-on-One Coaching Sessions:** Personalized sessions to help you identify and achieve your goals.

- **Goal Setting and Action Planning:** Develop a clear roadmap to success with actionable steps.

- **Mindset and Resilience Building:** Cultivate a positive and resilient mindset to navigate life's challenges.

- **Creative Problem Solving:** Learn innovative strategies to overcome obstacles and pursue your passions.

- **Support and Accountability:** Ongoing support to keep you motivated and accountable.

Ready to unlock your full potential with Derick Sebastian's life coaching services? Then schedule your complimentary consultation by contacting Derick below. Now is your time to create an inspiring and fulfilling life!

www.DerickSebastian.com

Team@DerickSebastian.com

(808) 870-8460

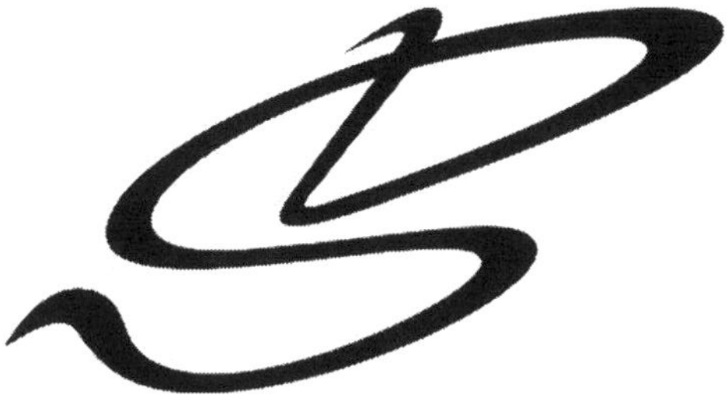

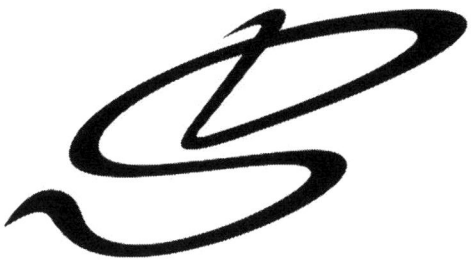

# BOOK DERICK SEBASTIAN AS A SPEAKER OR KEYNOTE PERFORMER

Through the pages of this book, you've seen the transformative power of resilience, creativity, and personal growth in Derick Sebastian's stories. Now, he is thrilled to bring these experiences to life through engaging keynote performances that combine inspirational stories with captivating ukulele music. This unique blend allows him to share his journey in a dynamic and memorable way, inspiring and motivating your audience to strive for their own goals. Whether it's a corporate event, conference, or special gathering, Derick's keynote performances are designed to leave a lasting impression and are filled with heartfelt narratives and uplifting melodies.

**Why Choose Derick Sebastian as Your Keynote Performer?**

- **Unique Blend of Storytelling and Music:** Experience a keynote performance that weaves together powerful narratives and uplifting ukulele performances.

- **Inspiration and Motivation:** Derick's journey of overcoming challenges and pursuing passions will inspire and motivate your audience to strive toward their own goals.

- **Engaging and Memorable:** The combination of heartfelt stories and live music creates a dynamic and memorable experience for any event

- **Tailored Presentations:** Each performance is customized to resonate with your audience and align with your event's theme and goals.

Keynote Performance Services:

- **Inspirational Keynote Speaking:** Share Derick's inspiring and empowering journey of resilience, creativity, and personal growth with your audience.

- **Ukulele Performances:** Enhance your event with live ukulele music, adding a unique and uplifting touch.

- **Customized Themes:** Tailor the presentation to fit the specific theme or objectives of your event, ensuring maximum effect and relevance.

- **Interactive Sessions:** Engage your audience with interactive elements, including Q&A sessions and audience participation.

Ready to create an inspiring and unforgettable experience at your next event? Book Derick Sebastian for a captivating keynote performance today! Don't miss this opportunity to inspire and motivate your audience with Derick's unique blend of storytelling and ukulele magic. To discuss how Derick can help make your event truly exceptional, contact him at:

www.DerickSebastian.com

Team@DerickSebastian.com

(808) 870-8460

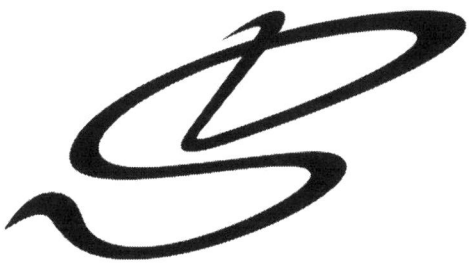

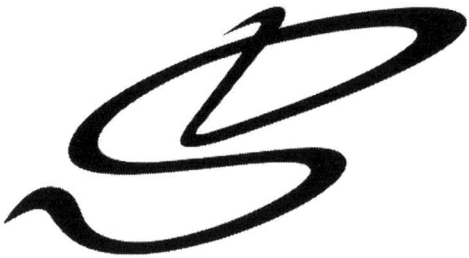

# MAHALO

Thank you for joining me on this journey. I truly appreciate your time, energy, and heart in reading my story. Your support means the world to me.

Please scan the QR code below for a personal Mahalo message.

www.DerickSebastian.com/Mahalo

Or

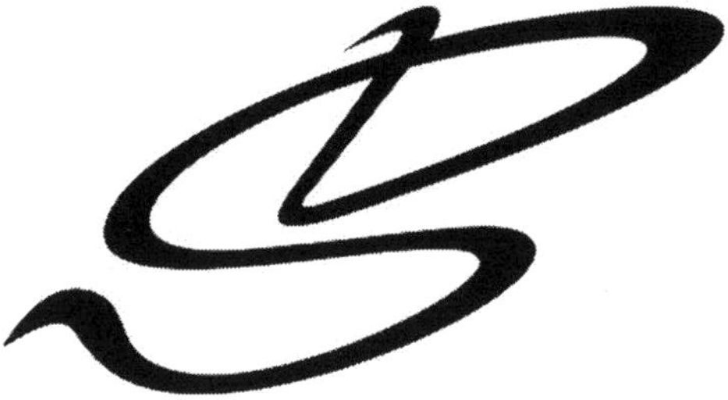

# THE STORY BEHIND THE STRINGS: FROM DREAMS TO REALITY

Explore the moments that shaped my life, music, and purpose.

Scan the QR code below to access the full photo insert and experience the memories behind the music.

www.DerickSebastian.com/PhotoInsert

Or

# NOTES